海外藏中国艺术品
OVERSEAS CHINESE ART SELECTION

绘画卷·清(一)
PAINTINGS · QING (1)

本书编写组 编著
Compiled by Editorial Team

郭怀宇 本卷主编
Edited by Guo Huaiyu

NEWSTAR PRESS
新星出版社

图书在版编目（CIP）数据

海外藏中国艺术品 . 绘画卷 . 清 . 一：汉英对照 / 郭怀宇主编；本书编写组编著 . -- 北京：新星出版社，2024.12

ISBN 978-7-5133-5446-2

Ⅰ . ①海… Ⅱ . ①郭… ②本… Ⅲ . ①中国画 – 中国 – 清代 – 图录 Ⅳ . ① K870.2

中国国家版本馆 CIP 数据核字 (2024) 第 056608 号

海外藏中国艺术品 绘画卷·清（一）

本书编写组　编　著
郭　怀　宇　本卷主编

责任编辑	李文彧	**特约编辑**	丁文文
英文审校	韩　华	**责任校对**	刘　义
装帧设计	冷暖儿	**责任印制**	李珊珊

出 版 人　马汝军
出版发行　新星出版社
　　　　　　（北京市西城区车公庄大街丙 3 号楼 8001　100044）
网　　址　www.newstarpress.com
法律顾问　北京市岳成律师事务所
印　　刷　河北尚唐印刷包装有限公司
开　　本　889mm×1194mm　1/16
印　　张　15
字　　数　375 千字
版　　次　2024 年 12 月第 1 版　2024 年 12 月第 1 次印刷
书　　号　ISBN 978-7-5133-5446-2
定　　价　328.00 元

版权专有，侵权必究。如有印装错误，请与出版社联系。
总机：010-88310888　　传真：010-65270449　　销售中心：010-88310811

出版说明

按中国文物学会统计，鸦片战争以来流失海外的中国文物超过一千万件。这些文物是中国文物重要而特殊的组成部分，除其历史、文化、艺术等方面价值，更因其所凝结的民族情感而备受各界关注。

近年来，中国政府积极推动文物追索，国内外学界也涌现出一批新的研究成果，文物流失研究方兴未艾。但受诸多因素限制，海外文物归国面临着许多实际困难，能追回的仍只是很少一部分。在此情况下，加强中外合作、开展联合研究，通过出版、数字化等方式让更多人有机会了解相关资料和研究成果，成了推动流失文物"活起来"、促进中华文化海外传播的一条可行路径。在国内外专家学者、文博机构等的支持下，新星出版社推出这套《海外藏中国艺术品》，希望能为广大读者及学者提供一套可资观赏、查阅和研究的参考读物。

《海外藏中国艺术品》出版之际，我们尤其希望通过这套书向林树中先生致敬。林树中先生自20世纪80年代起，花费近20年时间，自费走遍40多个国家和地区的200多所博物馆，呕心沥血、锲而不舍，记录了大量海外藏中国文物资料，编纂出版了《海外藏中国历代名画》，成为这一领域具有重大影响力的开创性成果。2013年，新星出版社联手林树中教授共同策划了《海外藏中国艺术品》项目，旨在全面整理他对流失海外的绘画、雕塑、书法、工艺品的丰富记录和研究成果。不幸的是，筹备工作开始不久，林树中教授因病辞世，这给整理与编纂工作带来巨大挑战，出版计划也因此被迫中断。

《海外藏中国艺术品》编纂出版的两大关键因素是专家学者的专业把关和海外藏品的图片授权。在重启并继续推动项目的过程中，我们重新组建了国内外专家组成的编纂团队，英国独角兽公司则协调许多知名博物馆向我们开放图片授权。合法取得文物图片使用授权后，编纂团队对入选文物加以鉴别与甄选，按时代顺序进行分卷、编排，并对文物中英文定名、创作时代、创作者、材质、规格等馆藏信息进行逐一确认。

《海外藏中国艺术品》共计20卷，收录文物2279件，来自海外33家知名博物馆，涵盖了铜器（2册）、陶瓷（3册）、书法（3册）、绘画（11册）和造像（1册）五大门类。

此次出版的《海外藏中国艺术品》因故未能收录金银器、玉器、服饰等艺术门类。我们愿以《海外藏中国艺术品》的出版为契机，努力搭建研究交流和成果出版发布平台，期待与国内外有关各方携手，共同推进流失文物领域相关工作，为中华优秀传统文化传承发展和中华文化国际传播作出新贡献。

囿于出版者水平，书中难免缺漏错讹之处，敬请专家、读者指正。

Preface

According to statistics from the Chinese Society of Cultural Relics, over ten million Chinese cultural relics have been dispersed overseas since the Opium War in the mid-19th century. They represent an important and unique part of China's cultural heritage. Beyond their historical, cultural, and artistic value, they are also of great interest to all sectors of society due to the national sentiments they embody.

In recent years, the Chinese government has been actively engaging in the recovery of Chinese cultural relics, and domestic and international academia has seen a surge in new research, making the study of the loss of Chinese cultural relics a burgeoning field. However, practical challenges have constrained the repatriation efforts, resulting in the recovery of only a small fraction of these relics. In light of this, it has become a feasible approach to enhance visibility and awareness of these artifacts through strengthened international cooperation, joint research, and the dissemination of materials and findings via publications and digitalization. With the support of domestic and international experts, scholars, cultural institutions, and museums, New Star Press has published the *Overseas Chinese Art Selection* series. This series aims to provide reference materials for readers and scholars to appreciate, consult, and study.

Upon the publication of this series, we would like to take this opportunity to pay tribute to Mr. Lin Shuzhong. Beginning in the 1980s, Lin devoted nearly two decades visiting over 200 museums in more than 40 countries and regions at his own expense. With remarkable dedication and perseverance, he documented a vast amount of information about Chinese cultural relics overseas and compiled and published *Famous Chinese Paintings Abroad*, which has become a groundbreaking work with significant influence in this field. In 2013, New Star Press collaborated with Professor Lin on *Overseas Chinese Art Selection*, aiming to comprehensively organize his extensive records and research on paintings, sculptures, calligraphy, and crafts lost overseas. Tragically, shortly after the preparatory work began, he passed away due to illness, presenting significant challenges to the project's continuation. As a result, the publication plan had to be suspended.

The successful compilation and publication of *Overseas Chinese Art Selection* depended on two critical factors: the professional scrutiny of experts and scholars and the license to use images granted by overseas museums. In the process of restarting the project, we set up a new compilation team composed of local and international experts. UK-based Unicorn Publishing Group LLP coordinated with many renowned overseas museums to secure permissions for image use. After legally obtaining their permissions, the compilation team appraised and selected artifacts, organized them into different categories and in chronological order, and confirmed collection information for each piece, including Chinese and English names, the time of creation, the artist's name, material, specifications, and other relevant information.

Overseas Chinese Art Selection consists of 20 volumes, with 2,279 cultural relics from 33 renowned museums overseas, covering five major categories: bronzes (two volumes), ceramics (three volumes), calligraphy (three volumes), paintings (11 volumes), and sculptures (one volume).

Categories such as gold and silver wares, jade wares, and costumes are not included. We hope this publication will help build a platform for research exchanges and publication of research findings. We are looking forward to working together with partners at home and abroad to jointly pursue initiatives related to lost Chinese cultural treasures, and contribute to the inheritance and development of China's excellent traditional culture and a wider knowledge of Chinese culture globally.

Despite our best efforts, errors and inaccuracies may be present due to the limitations of the publisher's expertise. We kindly invite experts and readers to point them out for further improvement.

凡例

一、《海外藏中国艺术品》绘画卷收录了宋、元、明、清代共 1178 件画作，每件画作由图片和中英文基本信息两部分组成。

二、本卷中画作依照时代分册：宋代 2 册，元代 1 册，明、清代各 4 册，共计 11 册。

三、本卷中具体画作顺序基本依照画家生卒年先后编排，同时兼顾风格、流派等相关因素。同一画家的画作如有准确年款，则依年款先后编排，无准确年款的画作基本按立轴、手卷、册页、扇面形制依序编排；传为某画家的画作，均编排在该画家画作最后。佚名画作均编排于各时代最后，并依人物、山水、花鸟等门类略作分类。

四、本卷中已有中文定名的画作名称，与官网名称不一致的，均依已有中文定名。

五、本卷中以朝代标明画作的时代信息，其相应的英文表述，统一注明朝代和具体起止时间，如"Ming dynasty (1368—1644)"。部分画作有准确年款，均注明。

六、本卷中画作的材质基本统一为纸本水墨、纸本设色、绢本水墨、绢本设色、绫本水墨、绫本设色六种，对应英文为 ink on paper, ink and color on paper, ink on silk, ink and color on silk, ink on satin, ink and color on satin。将 ink and touches of color on silk；ink, color, gold and silver on silk；ink and color on gold-flecked paper；ink and pale color on paper 等统一为以上相应材质。

七、本卷中画作的尺寸基本为画面尺寸，并注明了画面纵、横尺寸，对应英文为 H、W。

八、本卷充分尊重各海外博物馆的要求，将每幅画作的出处和图片版权信息均详细列出。但因该信息并非对画作本身的描述，故未翻译成中文。其中个别博物馆或美术馆，如大阪市立美术馆，未提供该信息，因此未收录。

Guide to the Reader

i. The paintings volume of *Overseas Chinese Art Selection* contains 1178 pieces of paintings from the Song (960-1279), Yuan (1271-1368), Ming (1368-1644) and Qing (1644-1911) dynasties. Each piece is accompanied by basic information in Chinese and English.

ii. The paintings are presented chronologically in eleven volumes, of which two volumes are for paintings from Song Dynasty, one volume including those of Yuan Dynasty, four volumes for those of Ming Dynasty and another four for paintings from Qing Dynasty.

iii. The order of the paintings within each dynasty generally follows the period of time when the artists lived, taking the artistic styles, genres, etc. into consideration. Paintings by the same artist are primarily sorted in accordance with the exact chronology information when known; otherwise, they are arranged in accordance with the form of the paintings, namely in the order of handing scroll, handscroll, album leaf, fan paintings. Paintings attributed to an uncertain artist, are placed at the very end of the composer's paintings. Anonymous paintings are sorted at the end of paintings of each dynasty in this volume in accordance with the category of figure, scenery, birds and flowers, etc.

iv. The established Chinese names of those paintings which may be given different names by the official website will be retained in this volume.

v. The era of the paintings is marked by the dynasty in the volume. Both the dynasty and specific starting and ending years of the dynasties are indicated in the English description, such as "Ming Dynasty (1368-1644)". The specific creating time of some paintings is already known, which has been presented clearly.

vi. The materials used in the paintings in this volume are primarily summarized into six types: namely ink on paper, ink and color on paper, ink on silk, ink and color on silk, ink on stain, ink and color on stain. While there are numerous varitions, such as ink and touches of color on silk; ink, color, gold and silver on silk; ink and color on gold-flecked paper; ink and pale color on paper; etc. These have been standardized to the above categories for consistency.

vii. Dimensions in the basic information of this volume primarily represent the size of the painting's image, with vertical measurements denoted by 'H' and horizontal measurements by 'W'.

viii. This volume fully respects the requirements of overseas museums, the credit line and image copyright of paintings provided by the museums have been listed in details. However, since such information is not a description of the paintings themselves, it is presented only in English. Some museums or galleries, such as The Osaka City Museum of Fine Arts, do not provide those information of the paintings when displaying them, therefore such information of some paintings is omitted here.

目　录
CONTENTS

清（一）
The Qing Dynasty（1）

1. 仿黄公望山水图 003
   Landscape After Huang Gongwang

2. 夏日山居图 004
   Mountain Village Embraced by Summer

3. 仿王蒙山水图 005
   Landscape After Wang Meng

4. 仿黄公望山水图 006
   Landscape After Huang Gongwang

5. 仿黄公望山水图 007
   Landscape After Huang Gongwang

6. 秋山图 008
   Autumn Hills

7. 仿古山水图册 009
   Landscapes After Old Masters

8. 仿董源夏山图 023
   Summer Mountains After Dong Yuan

9. 仿王蒙云壑松阴图 024
   Shade of Pines in Cloudy Valley After Wang Meng

10. 仿范宽溪亭山色图 025
    Mountain Scenery with Streams and Pavilions After Fan Kuan

11. 仿古山水图册 027
    Landscapes After Old Masters

12. 仿古山水图之仿杨升 033
    Landscape After Yang Sheng

13. 仿古山水图之仿董源 034
    Landscape After Dong Yuan

14. 仿古山水图之仿马琬 035
    Landscape After Ma Wan

15. 仿古山水图之仿倪瓒 036
    Landscape After Ni Zan

16. 仿古山水图之仿巨然 037
    Landscape After Ju Ran

17. 仿古山水图之仿范宽 038
    Landscape After Fan Kuan

18. 仿古山水图之仿王蒙 039
    Landscape After Wang Meng

19. 仿古山水图之仿惠崇 040
    Landscape After Hui Chong

20. 仿巨然溪山高士图 041
    Lofty Scholar Among Streams and Mountains After Ju Ran

21. 山水图 042
    Landscape

22. 仿古山水图 043
    Landscapes After Old Masters

23. 虞山图 055
    Scenery of Mount Yu

24. 仿赵大年山水图 057
    Landscape After Zhao Danian

25. 清初八大家为王揆作山水图册 059
    Landscapes Painted for Wang Kui

26. 仿黄公望山水图 063
    Landscape After Huang Gongwang

27. 太行山色图 065
    Colors of Mount Taihang

28. 仿黄公望富春山居图 067
    Dwelling in Fuchun Mountains After Huang Gongwang

29. 秋山行旅图 071
    Travelers in Autumn Mountains

30. 梅溪高隐图 072
    Lofty Hermit of Plum Creek

31. 仿王蒙修竹远山图 073
    Tall Bamboo and Distant Mountains After Wang Meng

32. 雨后晴峦图 .... 074 Mountains After Rain	52. 仿倪瓒山水图 .... 110 Landscape After Ni Zan
33. 仿李成雪景图 .... 075 Snowscape After Li Cheng	53. 仿王蒙溪山行旅图 .... 111 Travelers Among Streams and Mountains After Wang Meng
34. 松乔堂图 .... 077 Hall of Lofty Pines	54. 秋水图 .... 112 River in Autumn
35. 仙山楼阁图 .... 078 Pavilions in Mountains of Immortals	55. 万壑松风图 .... 113 Pine Wind from Myriad Villages
36. 仿燕文贵山水图 .... 081 Landscape After Yan Wengui	56. 没骨牡丹图 .... 114 Peonies
37. 山水图 .... 083 Landscape	57. 花卉图册 .... 115 Flower Paintings
38. 仿古诗意图册 .... 085 Album After Old Masters and Poems	58. 花卉图 .... 119 Carnations and Amaranthus
39. 溪山雨霁图 .... 087 Clearing After Rain over Streams and Mountains	59. 冷艳含香图 .... 120 Camellia and Wax Plum
40. 仿巨然山水图 .... 088 Deep in Mountains After Ju Ran	60. 仿钱选溪山早春图 .... 121 Stream and Mountain in Early Spring After Qian Xuan
41. 仿巨然烟浮远岫图 .... 089 Mist Floating on Distant Peak After Ju Ran	61. 柳岸牧牛图 .... 122 Buffalo on Willow Bank
42. 南都胜集图 .... 091 Landscape of Southern Capital	62. 仿李成古松图 .... 123 Old Pine After Li Cheng
43. 麓村高逸图 .... 092 Portrait of An Qi	63. 山水图 .... 124 Landscape
44. 仿吴镇山水图 .... 093 Landscape After Wu Zhen	64. 松涛图 .... 125 Soughing of Wind in Pines Echoes Melody of Spring
45. 仿黄公望山水图 .... 094 Landscape After Huang Gongwang	65. 春泉洗药图 .... 127 Cleansing Medicinal Herbs in Stream on Spring Day
46. 仿倪瓒秋山图 .... 095 Autumn Mountains After Ni Zan	66. 朱彝尊像 .... 128 Portrait of Zhu Yizun
47. 江国纶垂图 .... 097 Fishing in River Country at Blossom Time	67. 寒林图 .... 129 Landscape with Wintry Trees
48. 山水图 .... 099 Landscape	68. 仿李希古九如图 .... 130 Landscape After Li Xigu
49. 辋川图 .... 101 Wangchuan Villa	69. 芍药图 .... 131 White Peonies
50. 严滩春晓图 .... 107 Spring Morning at Yanling Shoals	70. 渡江图 .... 132 Crossing of Yangzi River
51. 仿黄公望山水图 .... 109 Landscape After Huang Gongwang	71. 山水图 .... 133 Landscape

#	中文	English	Page
72.	山水图	Landscape	134
73.	仿王蒙山水图	Landscape After Wang Meng	135
74.	山水图	Landscape	136
75.	黄檗宗僧侣群像	Portrait of Buddhist Monks of Obaku Sect	137
76.	仿黄公望浮岚暖翠图	Landscape After Huang Gongwang	139
77.	山水图	Landscape	142
78.	山水图	Landscape	143
79.	观瀑图	Landscape with Waterfall	144
80.	仿高克恭山水图	Landscape After Gao Kegong	145
81.	梅花书屋图	Plum Blossom Studio	146
82.	梅花图	Plum Blossoms	147
83.	仿梅花道人山水图	Landscape After Wu Zhen	148
84.	梅花图册	Plum Blossoms	149
85.	芝易东湖图卷	Lake Zhiyang and Eastern Lake	153
86.	断岗留别图	Farewell	155
87.	黄山八景图	Eight Views of Yellow Mountains	157
88.	荷塘花鸟图	Birds and Lotus Pond	165
89.	木瓜图	Quince	168
90.	菊花图	Chrysanthemum	169
91.	山水图册	Landscape Album	171
92.	鱼石图	Fish and Rocks	182
93.	双鹰图	Two Eagles	183
94.	仿天池道人荷花图	Lotus After Xu Wei	184
95.	仿郭恕先山水图	Landscape After Guo Shuxian	185
96.	荷塘戏禽图	Birds in Lotus Pond	187
97.	渔石图	Fish and Rocks	191
98.	书画合册	Paintings and Calligraphies	193
99.	草虫花卉图册	Flowers and Insects	207
100.	荷花水禽图	Lotus and Waterfowl	217
101.	诗画图册	Paintings and Poems	219
102.	山水图	Landscape	224
103.	四鱼图	Four Fish	225
	版权支持	Image Contributors	227
	编辑、出版人员	Editorial Staff	229

清（一）

The Qing Dynasty (1)

1. 仿黄公望山水图

明崇祯十一年（公元1638年）
王时敏
纸本水墨
立轴
纵59.6、横33.7厘米
耶鲁大学艺术博物馆

Landscape After Huang Gongwang

Late Ming to early Qing dynasty, dated 1638
Wang Shimin
Ink on paper
Hanging scroll
H×W : 59.6×33.7 cm
The Yale University Art Gallery
Leonard C. Hanna, Jr., Class of 1913, Fund

2. 夏日山居图

清顺治十六年（公元1659年）
王时敏
纸本水墨
立轴
纵156.2、横73厘米
克利夫兰美术馆

Mountain Village Embraced by Summer

Qing dynasty (1644–1911), dated 1659
Wang Shimin
Ink on paper
Hanging scroll
H×W : 156.2×73 cm
The Cleveland Museum of Art
Bequest of Mrs. A. Dean Perry 1997.104

3. 仿王蒙山水图

清康熙三年（公元1664年）
王时敏
纸本设色
立轴
纵219.8、横96.6厘米
芝加哥艺术博物馆

Landscape After Wang Meng

Qing dynasty (1644–1911), dated 1664
Wang Shimin
Ink and color on paper
Hanging scroll
H×W : 219.8×96.6 cm
The Art Institute of Chicago
Bertha Evans Brown Fund
© 2024. The Art Institute of Chicago / Art Resource, NY/ Scala, Florence

4. 仿黄公望山水图

清康熙五年（公元1666年）
王时敏
纸本水墨
立轴
纵134.6、横56.5厘米
大都会艺术博物馆

Landscape After Huang Gongwang

Qing dynasty (1644–1911), dated 1666
Wang Shimin
Ink on paper
Hanging scroll
H×W : 134.6×56.5 cm
The Metropolitan Museum of Art
Ex coll.: C. C. Wang Family, Gift of Douglas Dillon, 1980

5. 仿黄公望山水图

清康熙十六年（公元1677年）
王时敏
纸本设色
扇面
纵15.7、横49.5厘米
大都会艺术博物馆

Landscape After Huang Gongwang

Qing dynasty (1644–1911), dated 1677
Wang Shimin
Ink and color on paper
Fan
H×W : 15.7×49.5 cm
The Metropolitan Museum of Art
Bequest of John M. Crawford Jr., 1988

6. 秋山图

清
（传）王时敏
纸本水墨
立轴
纵87、横38.1厘米
费城艺术博物馆

Autumn Hills

Qing dynasty (1644–1911)
Attributed to Wang Shimin
Ink on paper
Hanging scroll
H×W : 87×38.1 cm
The Philadelphia Museum of Art
Gift of Hsiao Shou-ming, 1964
© 2024. Photo The Philadelphia Museum of Art/Art Resource/Scala, Florence

7. 仿古山水图册

清
王时敏、王翚
纸本设色
册页
每开：纵22、横33.8厘米
大都会艺术博物馆

Landscapes After Old Masters

Qing dynasty (1644–1911)
Wang Shimin and Wang Hui
Ink and color on paper
Album leaf
H×W(each leaf) : 22×33.8 cm
The Metropolitan Museum of Art
Purchase, The Dillon Fund Gift, 1989

山莊雪霽
倣右丞

甲寅之歲
奉常公索余作此冊公年方八十三雄今甲午已四十年
兩餘年六十三矣公之文孫秋崖捃討出以見示重
省前題跋深歎月之倏忽後有處于聲與君家三
世結筆墨之緣為不偶也時十月八日

石翁此冊作於康熙甲寅二月時年四十有三正銳意求
精沈湮於唐宋元明諸大家恰到好處時候又為烟翁
所命竭盡生平以成此冊非尋常數墨時可同年而語
計倣古十家共十二幀烟客寶之六於是年秋仲照倣十二
幅三年歲而後成益藏秘閣後歸烟客第四子也石翁跋內
文玘家傳之寶我在異公所書聞分書畫帳內拾閲信乎
王氏家傳之寶我在異公所書聞分書畫帳內拾閲信乎
帳內所存石谷卷冊共十五件此冊分在四房並註明首幅
蕭寺晚晴今恰有此冊在內且其閲分在申之歲石翁
於甲午年重跋筆隔卅餘歲謂秋崖拾討出以見示年代
房分亦皆相符其為當年世寶答疑惜烟客十二幅僅
存其二而石翁十二幅古雲分古仿花中立黃子久兩
幅其主其閣盜遺兵燹殘玉同歸於爐可慨此冊余
偶人斯而究抑何可恨然此等寶物鬼神所嫉天地所嫉
開太璞不完抑何可恨然此等寶物鬼神所嫉天地所嫉
細按賓鑒參章自太倉陸氏賺藏後不數十年而已三
仍以蕭寺晚晴冠首後其舊製附烟客二幅稜以
何人斯而竟得此顔少留缺陷以免造物之忌云兩今
識前人彼此相師一段佳話
同治四年乙丑菊月廿一日西園主人識於大蘇小米之屏
兩穎盦的是國初人筆墨拔開張於首跋
園章聽㝡二字是陸氏次孫其名闕另所題跋

同治九年庚午端陽日友人朱芝甫別駕攜煙客畫冊十開見示云即余所藏之妖也展閱之倣諸家小景與石谷子畫本大半相同而署款之字跡若老摸糊印章之別抉六与所在及果惟冊後另趙畝行與畫尾拕敘月分少有參差未能遽信惹取石谷冊校對始兒兩賢全璧樓其年月當是石谷子為烟翁倣古烟范照倣十二開因年邁目眵于細瓷精緻寬不能著手牧中有六幅照倣餘或用原稿而變換之我別撰他之為倣趙㧾波蕭寺晚晴根翁沙磧及晴𡾋晚色倣巨師空山古栂趙大年平林薂牧李咸熙寒林六幅一樣而其閒六少有不同蕭寺晚晴一幅右邊沙磧少數層中峯下兩漁舟未盡青綠加重沙磧一幅綵色較濃倣巨師一幅石下村栂楷稀平林薂乘陰破竹趣圖金剛政倣荊開戴宮用墨華寫意高尚書堂山齋其位置化雲芳氣香綠加濃趙令穰桃花漁政穵寂木乘陰設色寫高少荒中立王右丞兩家另倣倪高士溪山亭子梅道人樹石是文指照倣中而自著變化也合觀二冊一則秀色可餐一則苍筆纔誠為兩賢極得意之作倘歸一人豈非快事乃烟容一冊今為嘉興張武翔伯所得其人茗張姝末族弘志知謂收藏年少小康恓一時未能合璧而彼恛才十用寒林夏木二開在余𠷢余所石谷冊文少二開六天塊閒一大缺陷也

附烟客尾題

余自指力向衰蒙筆情觀久殊監辨此多疴日日逢風日清美道来舎咸倣諸家小景積久戍冊頗用自喜蓋冯小如原祁謂遷入都學筭若年长果世至誼於光若栄之以為孺子利兒之資還以并之仰元六方郢政卿當親永指誨知醍廻不堪嶽嘆也庚戌乙巳夏五㑚敏彖題時年九十有六

8. 仿董源夏山图

明崇祯十五年（公元1642年）
王鉴
纸本水墨
立轴
纵171、横91厘米
波士顿美术博物馆

Summer Mountains After Dong Yuan

Late Ming to early Qing dynasty, dated 1642
Wang Jian
Ink on paper
Hanging scroll
H×W : 171×91 cm
The Museum of Fine Arts, Boston
Gift of the Wan-go H. C. Weng Collection and the Weng family, in memory of Virginia Dzung Weng
© 2024 Museum of Fine Arts, Boston

9. 仿王蒙云壑松阴图

清顺治十七年（公元1660年）
王鉴
纸本水墨
立轴
纵128.2、横61厘米
克利夫兰美术馆

Shade of Pines in Cloudy Valley After Wang Meng

Qing dynasty (1644–1911), dated 1660
Wang Jian
Ink on paper
Hanging scroll
H×W : 128.2×61 cm
The Cleveland Museum of Art
Bequest of Mrs. A. Dean Perry

10. 仿范宽溪亭山色图

清康熙六年（公元1667年）
王鉴
纸本设色
立轴
纵86.4、横44.5厘米
大都会艺术博物馆

Mountain Scenery with Streams and Pavilions After Fan Kuan

Qing dynasty (1644–1911), dated 1667
Wang Jian
Ink and color on paper
Hanging scroll
H×W : 86.4×44.5 cm
The Metropolitan Museum of Art
Gift of Franklin Z. Davidson, MD and Carol R. Fishberg, 2015

11. 仿古山水图册

清康熙七年（公元1668年）
王鉴
纸本设色
册页
每开：纵25.7、横16.5厘米
大都会艺术博物馆

Landscapes After Old Masters

Qing dynasty (1644–1911), dated 1668
Wang Jian
Ink and color on paper
Album leaf
H×W(each leaf) : 25.7×16.5 cm
The Metropolitan Museum of Art
Purchase, The Dillon Fund Gift, 1979

余三十年前主虞山錢牧翁先生上得交馨之道人見其評論法書名畫及三代彝鼎羲如指掌列眉不爽毫髮後余移居金閶每同一古玩居之鑒賞相與印證時皆少壯興致勃勃俱自頭藏晚余則貧病杜門馨老則寄居蕭寺兩人暮年失意不減杜陵老比不畫特迎之過甚度歲盤桓匝月相過甚歡於其告歸不禁臨歧念念以為贈染

軾倣古十幀樂老偶有金陵集遂取其句中與境合者題之於左恨之畫中有詩深愧古人比但馨老不善步履當此冊聊當臥遊耳

戊申春二月婁東王鑑識

12. 仿古山水图之仿杨升

清康熙八年（公元1669年）
王鉴
纸本设色
册页
纵21.1、横14.1厘米
耶鲁大学艺术博物馆

Landscape After Yang Sheng

Qing dynasty (1644–1911), dated 1669
Wang Jian
Ink and color on paper
Album leaf
H×W : 21.1×14.1 cm
The Yale University Art Gallery
Leonard C. Hanna, Jr., Class of 1913, Fund

13. 仿古山水图之仿董源 — Landscape After Dong Yuan

清康熙八年（公元1669年）
王鉴
纸本水墨
册页
纵21.6、横14.6厘米
耶鲁大学艺术博物馆

Qing dynasty (1644–1911), dated 1669
Wang Jian
Ink on paper
Album leaf
H×W : 21.6×14.6 cm
The Yale University Art Gallery
Leonard C. Hanna, Jr., Class of 1913, Fund

14. 仿古山水图之仿马琬

清康熙八年（公元1669年）
王鉴
纸本设色
册页
纵21.6、横14.6厘米
耶鲁大学艺术博物馆

Landscape After Ma Wan

Qing dynasty (1644–1911), dated 1669
Wang Jian
Ink and color on paper
Album leaf
H×W: 21.6×14.6 cm
The Yale University Art Gallery
Leonard C. Hanna, Jr., Class of 1913, Fund

15. 仿古山水图之仿倪瓒

清康熙八年（公元1669年）
王鉴
纸本水墨
册页
纵21.6、横14.6厘米
耶鲁大学艺术博物馆

Landscape After Ni Zan

Qing dynasty (1644–1911), dated 1669
Wang Jian
Ink on paper
Album leaf
H×W : 21.6×14.6 cm
The Yale University Art Gallery
Leonard C. Hanna, Jr., Class of 1913, Fund

16. 仿古山水图之仿巨然

清康熙八年（公元1669年）
王鉴
纸本水墨
册页
纵21.6、横14.6厘米
耶鲁大学艺术博物馆

Landscape After Ju Ran

Qing dynasty (1644–1911), dated 1669
Wang Jian
Ink on paper
Album leaf
H×W : 21.6×14.6 cm
The Yale University Art Gallery
Leonard C. Hanna, Jr., Class of 1913, Fund

17. 仿古山水图之仿范宽

清康熙八年（公元1669年）
王鉴
纸本设色
册页
纵21.6、横14.6厘米
耶鲁大学艺术博物馆

Landscape After Fan Kuan

Qing dynasty (1644–1911), dated 1669
Wang Jian
Ink and color on paper
Album leaf
H×W : 21.6×14.6 cm
The Yale University Art Gallery
Leonard C. Hanna, Jr., Class of 1913, Fund

18. 仿古山水图之仿王蒙

清康熙八年（公元1669年）
王鉴
纸本水墨
册页
纵21.6、横14.6厘米
耶鲁大学艺术博物馆

Landscape After Wang Meng

Qing dynasty (1644–1911), dated 1669
Wang Jian
Ink on paper
Album leaf
H×W : 21.6×14.6 cm
The Yale University Art Gallery
Leonard C. Hanna, Jr., Class of 1913, Fund

19. 仿古山水图之仿惠崇

清康熙八年（公元1669年）
王鉴
纸本设色
册页
纵21.6、横14.6厘米
耶鲁大学艺术博物馆

Landscape After Hui Chong

Qing dynasty (1644–1911), dated 1669
Wang Jian
Ink and color on paper
Album leaf
H×W : 21.6×14.6 cm
The Yale University Art Gallery
Leonard C. Hanna, Jr., Class of 1913, Fund

20. 仿巨然溪山高士图

清
王鉴
纸本水墨
立轴
纵182.9、横83.8厘米
大都会艺术博物馆

Lofty Scholar Among Streams and Mountains After Ju Ran

Qing dynasty (1644–1911)
Wang Jian
Ink on paper
Hanging scroll
H×W : 182.9×83.8 cm
The Metropolitan Museum of Art
Gift of Douglas Dillon, 1991

21. 山水图 — Landscape

清
王鉴
绢本设色
立轴
尺寸不详
芝加哥艺术博物馆

Qing dynasty (1644–1911)
Wang Jian
Ink and color on silk
Hanging scroll
Dimensions unknown
The Art Institute of Chicago
Bertha Evans Brown Purchase Fund
© 2024. The Art Institute of Chicago / Art Resource, NY/ Scala, Florence

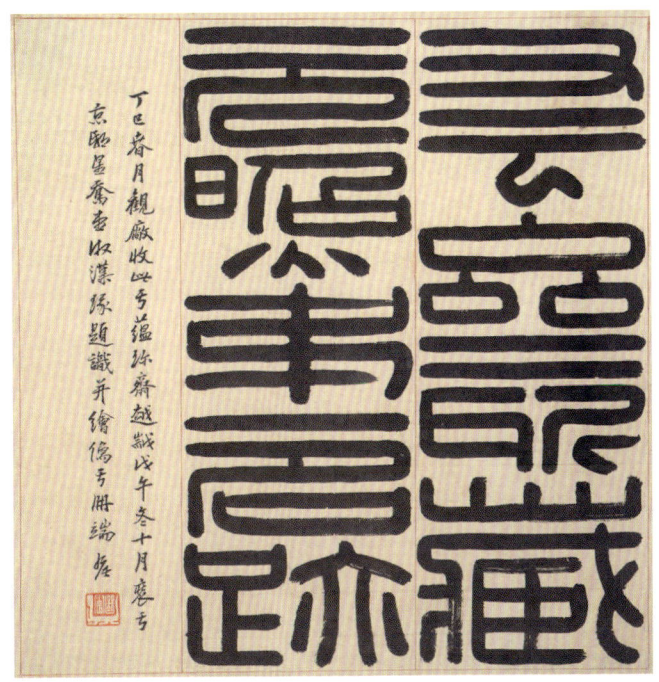

22. 仿古山水图

清
王鉴
纸本设色
册页
每开：纵29.8、横31.4厘米
大都会艺术博物馆

Landscapes After Old Masters

Qing dynasty (1644–1911)
Wang Jian
Ink and color on paper
Album leaf
H×W(each leaf) : 29.8×31.4 cm
The Metropolitan Museum of Art
Edward Elliott Family Collection, Gift of
Douglas Dillon Gift, 1989

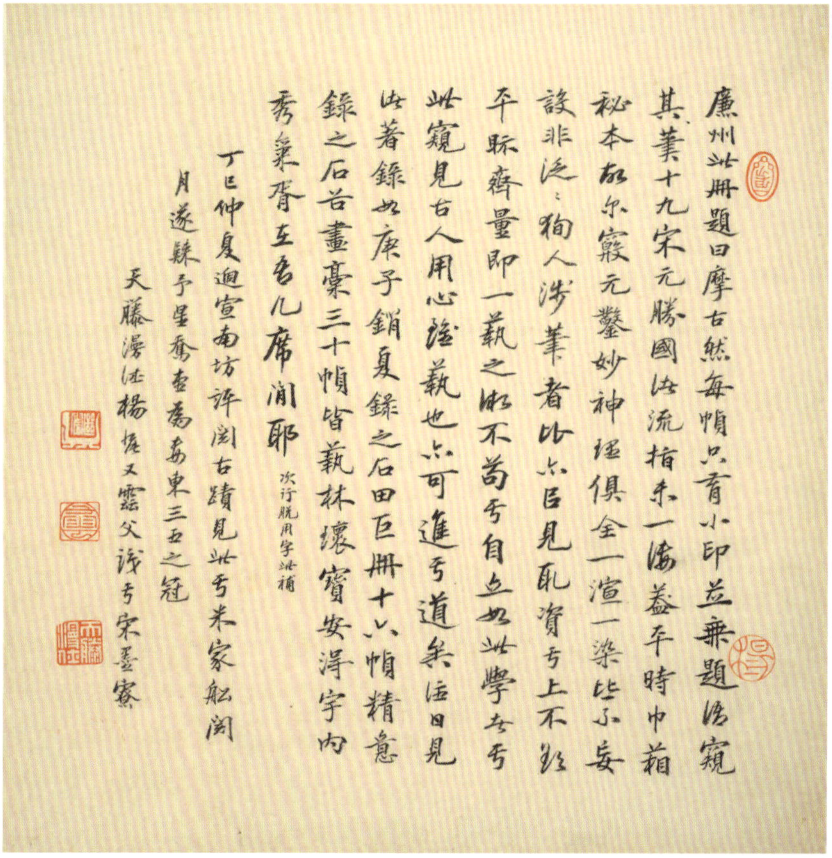
廉州此册題曰摩古然每幀只有小印並無題識竊
其葉十九宋元勝國諸流指不一法蓋平時巾箱
秘本故爾竅元鑿妙神理俱全一渲一染皆不妄
設非泛泛狗人涉筆者比亦足見乳資于上不淺
平昕齋量即一藝之微不苟于自立如此學者于
此竊見古人用心雖藝也亦可進于道矣往日見
此著錄如庚子銷夏錄之石田巨册十八幀精意
錄之石谷畫豪三十幀皆藝林瓌寶安得宇內
秀氣聚脊在吾几席間耶 次行脫用字此補
丁巳仲夏過宣南坊評閱古蹟見此于米家船閣
月遂購予星喬查舊安東三五之冠
天藤湯沐楊[illegible]又霑父識于宋墨寮

23. 虞山图

清康熙元年（公元1662年）
（传）王鉴
纸本水墨
手卷
纵30.8、横441.2厘米
辛辛那提艺术博物馆

Scenery of Mount Yu

Qing dynasty (1644–1911), dated 1662
Attributed to Wang Jian
Ink on paper
Handscroll
H×W : 30.8×441.2 cm
The Cincinnati Art Museum
John J. Emery Endowment and The Edwin and Virginia Irwin Memorial
© Bridgeman Images

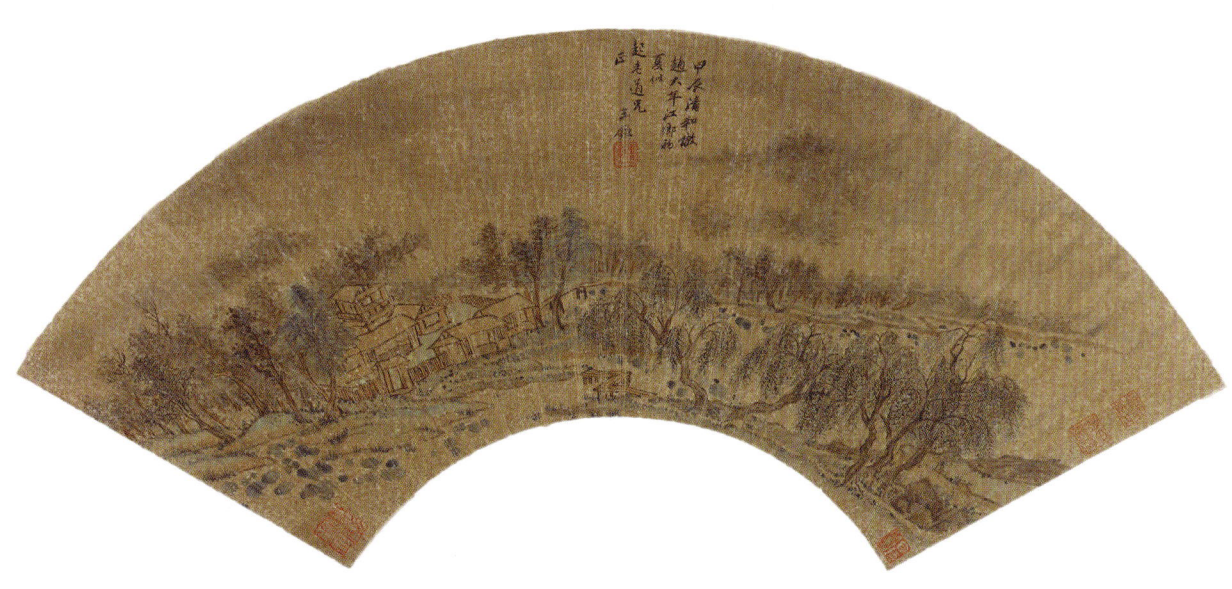

24. 仿赵大年山水图

清康熙三年（公元1664年）
（传）王鉴
纸本设色
扇面
纵33.02、横60.96厘米
印第安纳波利斯艺术博物馆

Landscape After Zhao Danian

Qing dynasty (1644–1911), dated 1664
Attributed to Wang Jian
Ink and color on paper
Fan
H×W : 33.02×60.96 cm
The Indianapolis Museum of Art
Gift of Sonia and Joseph Lesser

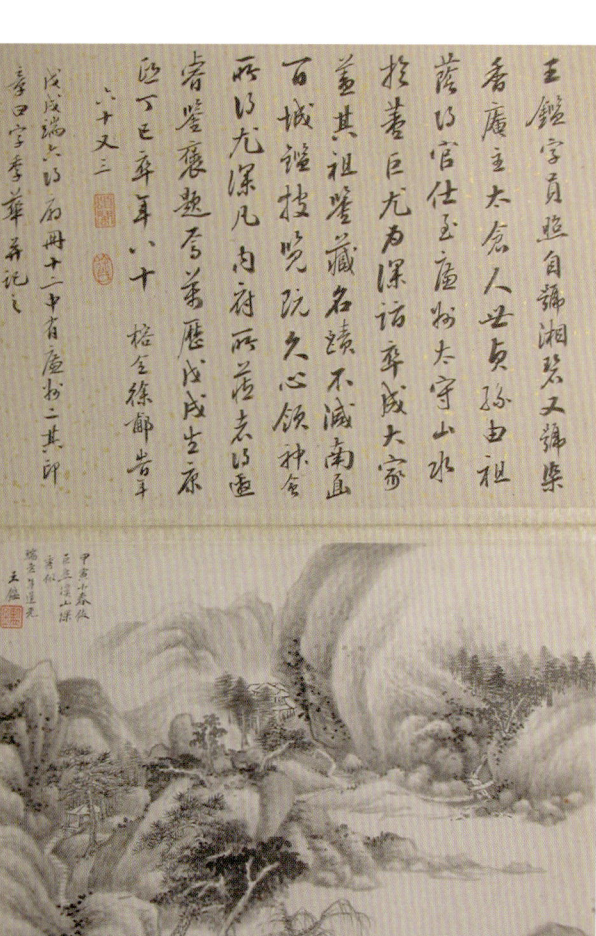

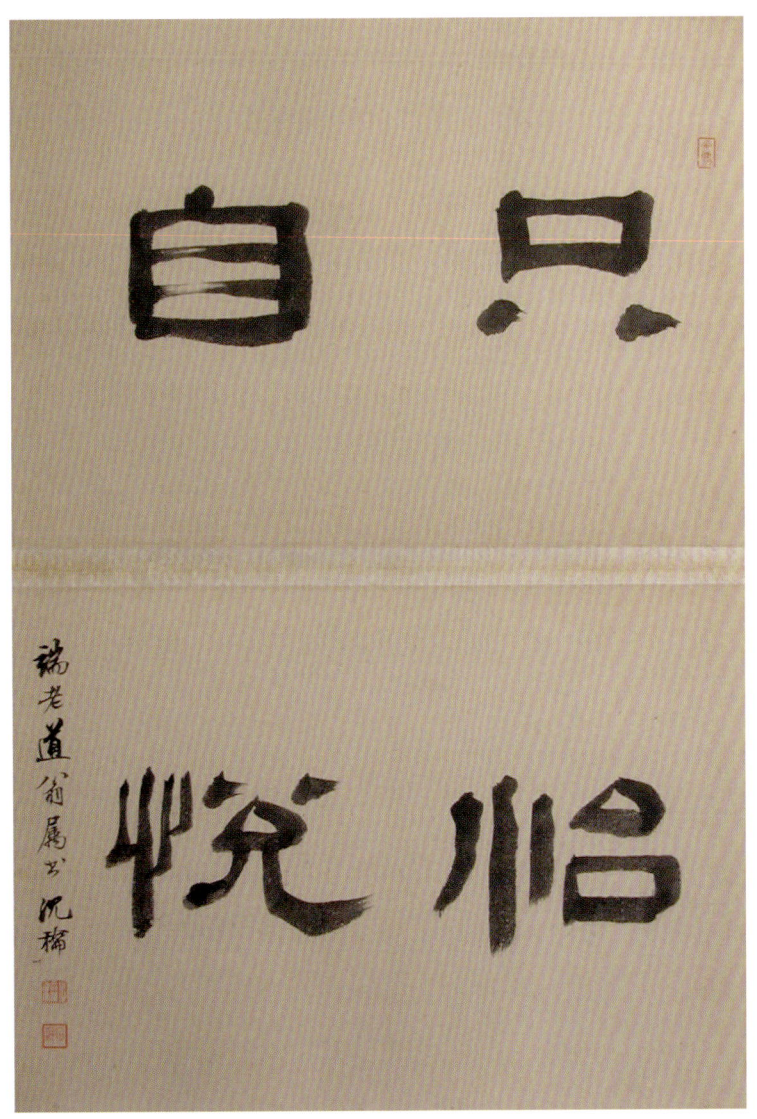

25. 清初八大家为王撰作山水图册

清
王鉴、吴历、童璘、高简、
朱陵、张适、金侃、沈琅
纸本设色
册页
每开：纵31.1、横22.9厘米
大都会艺术博物馆

Landscapes Painted for Wang Kui

Qing dynasty (1644–1911)
Wang Jian, Wu Li, Tong Bin, Gao Jian,
Zhu Jun, Zhang Shi, Jin Kan, Shen Lang
Ink and color on paper
Album leaf
H×W(each leaf): 31.1×22.9 cm
The Metropolitan Museum of Art
Gift of Douglas Dillon, 1979

張道字鈞民號梅莊吳人
梅花山水俱蒼老法秀逸
圖繪寶鑑續纂 櫄園居人

金保字忘陶偹明子又號立
養传其植花童长青綠山
水乃黄珏泓工李能詩杜門
不出搜雙典籍多蓄宋元
秘本 麈淑詞 徐郁甫当年六十
有三

26. 仿黄公望山水图   Landscape After Huang Gongwang

清顺治十七年（公元1660年）
王翚
纸本水墨
立轴
纵174、横89.6厘米
普林斯顿大学美术馆

Qing dynasty (1644–1911), dated 1660
Wang Hui
Ink on paper
Hanging scroll
H×W : 174×89.6 cm
The Princeton University Art Museum
Gift of Mr. and Mrs. Earl Morse, in honor of Wen C. Fong, Class of 1951 and Graduate School Class of 1958, and Constance Tang Fong
© 2024. Princeton University Art Museum/Art Resource NY/Scala, Florence

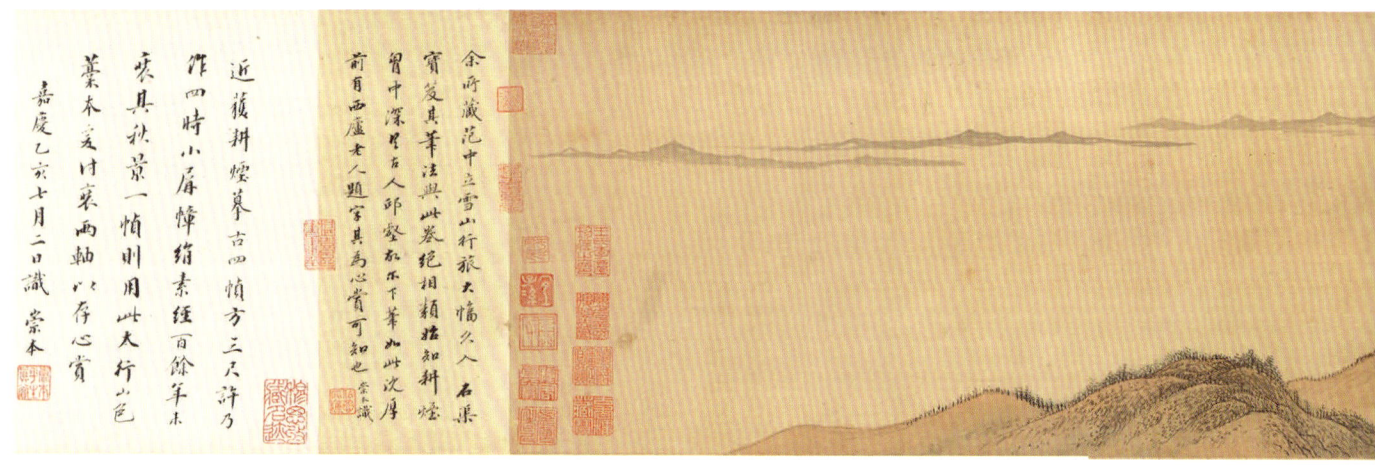

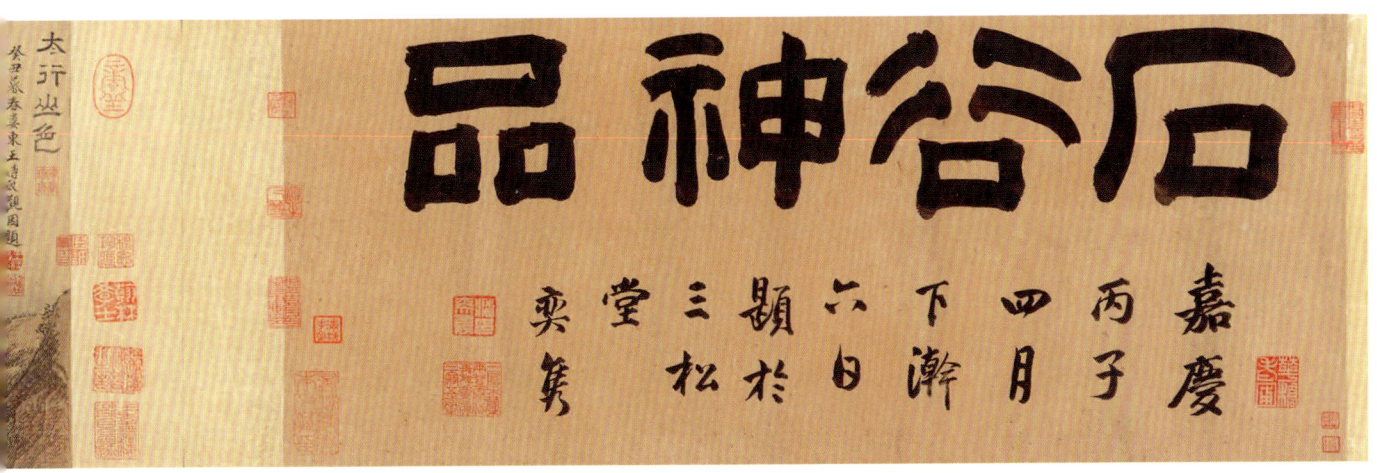

27. 太行山色图

清康熙八年（公元1669年）
王翚
绢本设色
手卷
纵25.3、横209.4厘米
大都会艺术博物馆

Colors of Mount Taihang

Qing dynasty (1644–1911), dated 1669
Wang Hui
Ink and color on silk
Handscroll
H×W : 25.3×209.4 cm
The Metropolitan Museum of Art
Ex coll.: C. C. Wang Family, Gift of Douglas Dillon, 1978

28. 仿黄公望富春山居图 — Dwelling in Fuchun Mountains After Huang Gongwang

清康熙十一年（公元1672年）
王翚
纸本设色
手卷
纵38.4、横743厘米
弗利尔美术馆

Qing dynasty (1644–1911), dated 1672
Wang Hui
Ink and color on paper
Handscroll
H×W : 38.4×743 cm
The Freer Gallery of Art
Purchase—Charles Lang Freer Endowment

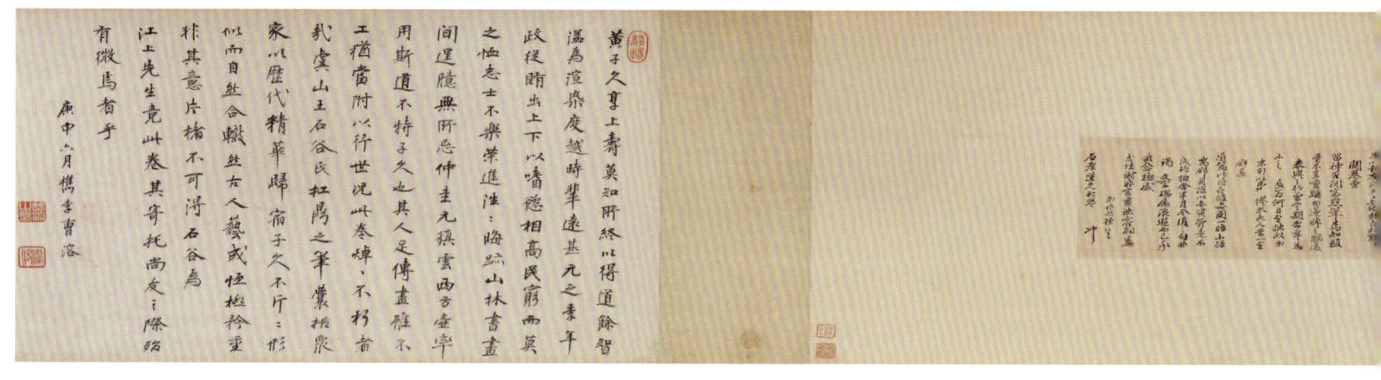

29. 秋山行旅图

清康熙十八年（公元1679年）
王翚
绢本设色
立轴
纵152.4、横78.7厘米
耶鲁大学艺术博物馆

Travelers in Autumn Mountains

Qing dynasty (1644–1911), dated 1679
Wang Hui
Ink and color on silk
Hanging scroll
H×W : 152.4×78.7 cm
The Yale University Art Gallery
Gift of David Y. Wong in memory of Wong Nan-p'ing

30. 梅溪高隐图

清康熙二十七年（公元1688年）
王翚
纸本水墨
立轴
纵74.1、横33.8厘米
弗利尔美术馆

Lofty Hermit of Plum Creek

Qing dynasty (1644–1911), dated 1688
Wang Hui
Ink on paper
Hanging scroll
H×W : 74.1×33.8 cm
The Freer Gallery of Art
Transfer from the United States Customs Service, Department of the Treasury

31. 仿王蒙修竹远山图

清康熙三十三年（公元1694年）
王翚
纸本水墨
立轴
纵79.3、横39.5厘米
克利夫兰美术馆

Tall Bamboo and Distant Mountains After Wang Meng

Qing dynasty (1644–1911), dated 1694
Wang Hui
Ink on paper
Hanging scroll
H×W : 79.3×39.5 cm
The Cleveland Museum of Art
John L. Severance Fund 1953.629

32. 雨后晴峦图

清康熙三十四年（公元1695年）
王翚
纸本设色
扇面
纵16.4、横49.2厘米
大都会艺术博物馆

Mountains After Rain

Qing dynasty (1644–1911), dated 1695
Wang Hui
Ink and color on paper
Fan
H×W : 16.4×49.2 cm
The Metropolitan Museum of Art
Bequest of John M. Crawford Jr., 1988

33. 仿李成雪景图

清康熙三十五年（公元1696年）
王翚
纸本设色
立轴
纵43.4、横50.2厘米
弗利尔美术馆

Snowscape After Li Cheng

Qing dynasty (1644–1911), dated 1696
Wang Hui
Ink and color on paper
Hanging scroll
H×W : 43.4×50.2 cm
The Freer Gallery of Art
Purchase—Charles Lang Freer Endowment

原余題弥其後余興公同官傳紀交斿家

深側見公之清修純德蔚為

聖天子所眷重倚直

內廷密勿贊襄幾二十餘年蒼生之所以受賜士

林之所以沐德者天下莫能窺在建莫能卷而

公平不言以故

宸衷日益契恩禮日益隆雖年餘懸車時有

歸老之念而

上固不曉公之去其所謂松喬堂者

御書以賜公者也蓋以松比公之清風勁節而歲寒

不改經霜弥茂則又以期公之壽考未艾

艾烏以知此身未易乞而山林槃礀之樂也

可寄諸宿里此松喬堂之所由作也歟石

谷此圖結構精密筆墨超邁甚寓樹木之

蒼蔚堂宇之靚幽恍見摩詰輞川樂天廬

山之勝猶惜公之未得以永其趣此緇修天之

願助繪松園云未得也雖然千歲之松喬下蔭百畝

所以卷之永忘也即一日徜徉故周以償其

上以僑棟梁之霓笠則

上有日命堂之意不更摯於茂之人蓺其茂而

養其枝業我主顧緇修天之寶斯圖矣

望君之塗堼丹雘以大其堂搆之云夫

康熙丙戌重陽後三日雲間王鴻緒跋

34. 松乔堂图

清康熙四十二年（公元1703年）
王翚
纸本水墨
手卷
纵：40.7厘米
克利夫兰美术馆

Hall of Lofty Pines

Qing dynasty (1644–1911), dated 1703
Wang Hui
Ink on paper
Handscroll
H: 40.7 cm
The Cleveland Museum of Art
Bequest of Mrs. A. Dean Perry

35. 仙山楼阁图

清康熙五十一年（公元1712年）
王翚
纸本设色
立轴
纵175.5、横36.2厘米
赛克勒美术馆

Pavilions in Mountains of Immortals

Qing dynasty (1644–1911), dated 1712
Wang Hui
Ink and color on paper
Hanging scroll
H×W : 175.5×36.2 cm
The Arthur M. Sackler Gallery
Gift of Arthur M. Sackler

36. 仿燕文贵山水图

清康熙五十二年（公元1713年）
王翚
纸本设色
手卷
纵31.1、横402.3厘米
大都会艺术博物馆

Landscape After Yan Wengui

Qing dynasty (1644–1911), dated 1713
Wang Hui
Ink and color on paper
Handscroll
H×W : 31.1×402.3 cm
The Metropolitan Museum of Art
Ex coll.: C. C. Wang Family, Gift of Douglas Dillon, 1979

37. 山水图

清
王翚
绢本设色
立轴
纵200.9、横99.2厘米
克利夫兰美术馆

Landscape

Qing dynasty (1644–1911)
Wang Hui
Ink and color on silk
Hanging scroll
H×W：200.9×99.2 cm
The Cleveland Museum of Art
Gift of Charles L. Freer

38. 仿古诗意图册

清
王翚
纸本水墨
册页
每开：纵33.02、横30.48厘米
印第安纳波利斯艺术博物馆

Album After Old Masters and Poems

Qing dynasty (1644–1911)
Wang Hui
Ink on paper
Album leaf
H×W(each leaf)：33.02×30.48 cm
The Indianapolis Museum of Art
Thomas W. Ayton Fund

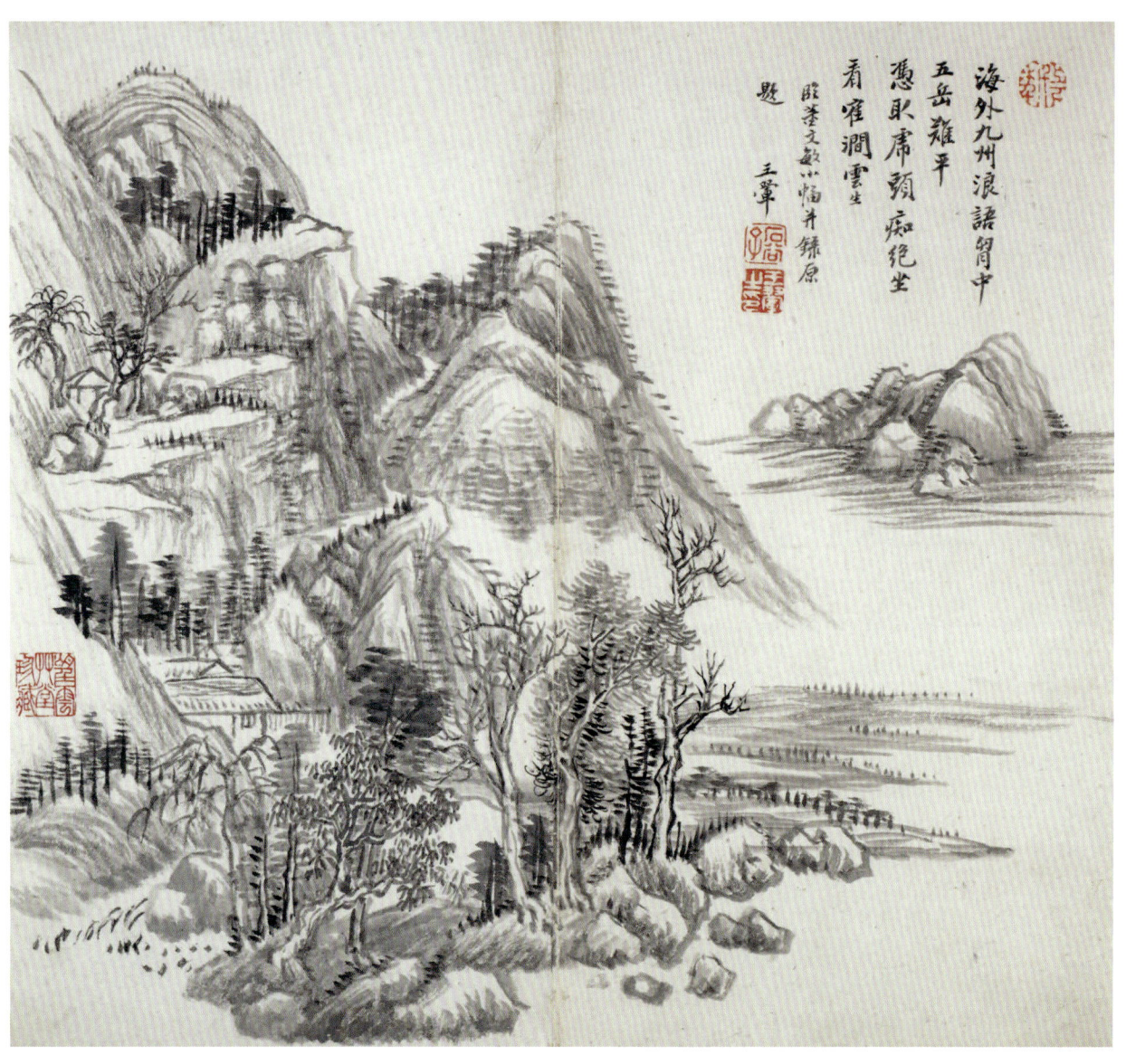

39. 溪山雨霁图

清康熙元年（公元1662年）
（传）王翚
纸本水墨
立轴
纵114、横45.4厘米
大都会艺术博物馆

Clearing After Rain over Streams and Mountains

Qing dynasty (1644–1911), dated 1662
Attributed to Wang Hui
Ink on paper
Hanging scroll
H×W : 114×45.4 cm
The Metropolitan Museum of Art
Bequest of John M. Crawford Jr., 1988

40. 仿巨然山水图

清康熙三十一年（公元1692年）
（传）王翚
纸本设色
立轴
纵111、横48.5厘米
科隆东亚艺术博物馆

Deep in Mountains After Ju Ran

Qing dynasty (1644–1911), dated 1692
Attributed to Wang Hui
Ink and color on paper
Hanging scroll
H×W : 111×48.5 cm
The Museum of East Asian Art, Cologne
© Rheinisches Bildarchiv Köln

41. 仿巨然烟浮远岫图   **Mist Floating on Distant Peak After Ju Ran**

清
（传）王翚
绢本水墨
立轴
纵193、横71.5厘米
普林斯顿大学美术馆

Qing dynasty (1644–1911)
Attributed to Wang Hui
Ink on silk
Hanging scroll
H×W : 193×71.5 cm
The Princeton University Art Museum
Gift of Mr. and Mrs. Earl Morse
© 2024. Princeton University Art Museum/Art Resource NY/Scala, Florence

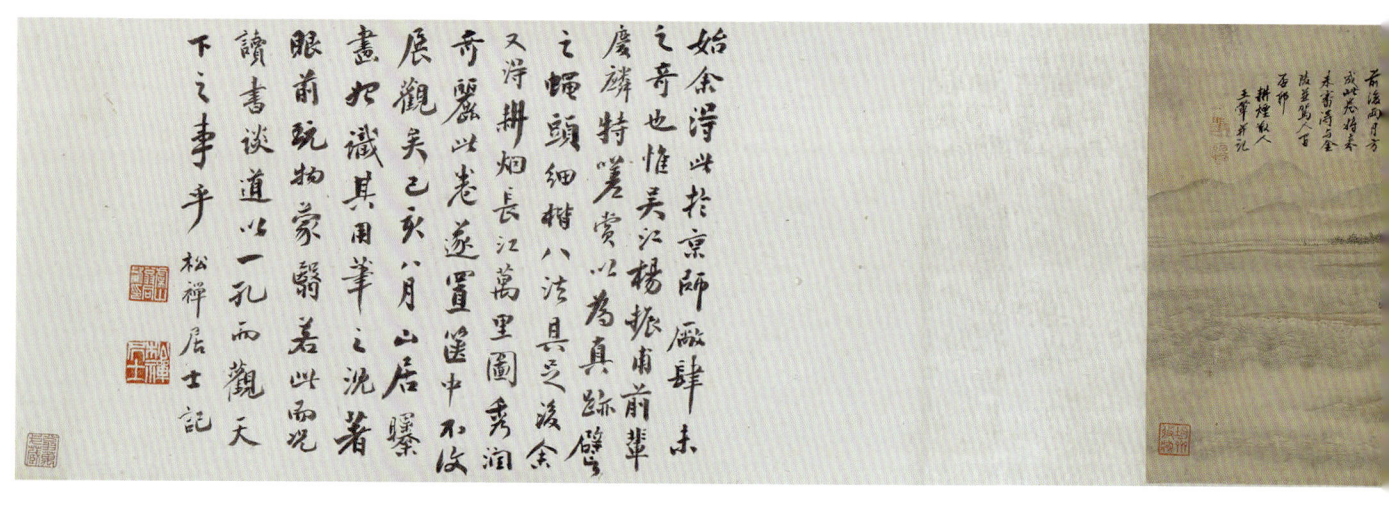

始余浮也於京師廠肆未
之奇也惟吳江楊振甫前輩
鏖麟特甞賞以為真跡啓
之幅頭細楷八法具之後余
又得冊烟長江萬里圖秀潤
奇麗以卷遂置篋中加汶
展觀矣己亥八月山居驟
畫如識其用筆之洗著
眼前玩物豪翳若此兩悦
讀書談道以一孔而觀天
下之事手 松禪居士記

42. 南都胜集图

清康熙四十二年（公元1703年）
（传）王翚
绢本设色
手卷
纵25.1、横261.5厘米
波士顿美术博物馆

Landscape of Southern Capital

Qing dynasty (1644–1911), dated 1703
Attributed to Wang Hui
Ink and color on silk
Handscroll
H×W : 25.1×261.5 cm
The Museum of Fine Arts, Boston
Gift of the Wan-go H. C. Weng Collection and the Weng family, in memory of Virginia Dzung Weng
© 2024 Museum of Fine Arts, Boston

43. 麓村高逸图

清康熙五十四年（公元1715年）
王翚、杨晋、涂洛
纸本设色
立轴
纵121.8、横53.5厘米
克利夫兰美术馆

Portrait of An Qi

Qing dynasty (1644–1911), dated 1715
Wang Hui, Yang Jin, Tu Luo
Ink and color on paper
Hanging scroll
H×W : 121.8×53.5 cm
The Cleveland Museum of Art
John L. Severance Fund

44. 仿吴镇山水图

清康熙三十四年（公元1695年）
王原祁
纸本水墨
立轴
纵108.6、横51.4厘米
大都会艺术博物馆

Landscape After Wu Zhen

Qing dynasty (1644–1911), dated 1695
Wang Yuanqi
Ink on paper
Hanging scroll
H×W : 108.6×51.4 cm
The Metropolitan Museum of Art
Bequest of John M. Crawford Jr., 1988

45. 仿黄公望山水图

Landscape After Huang Gongwang

清康熙四十年（公元1701年）
王原祁
纸本水墨
立轴
尺寸不详
芝加哥艺术博物馆

Qing dynasty (1644–1911), dated 1701
Wang Yuanqi
Ink on paper
Hanging scroll
Dimensions unknown
The Art Institute of Chicago
Gift of Hulburd Johnston
© 2024. The Art Institute of Chicago / Art Resource, NY/ Scala, Florence

46. 仿倪瓒秋山图

清康熙四十三年（公元1704年）
王原祁
纸本设色
立轴
纵95.9、横50.6厘米
弗利尔美术馆

Autumn Mountains After Ni Zan

Qing dynasty (1644–1911), dated 1704
Wang Yuanqi
Ink and color on paper
Hanging scroll
H×W : 95.9×50.6 cm
The Freer Gallery of Art
Purchase—Charles Lang Freer Endowment

余家舊藏子金畫册有松雪花溪漁隱一幅青山
碧湖桃花四面小舟一人高梁中流最為神逸之筆
思翁易為長幅作江上景臨同用夏山筆法綠
蔭周遶流漸水草人柔谕小觥禾是此卷而作用
五黛年己丑九秋積雨初晴造名事稍鞖追憶內
園山膝見鞖戊寒甬成為 兩長世兄示見托
友將素紙郭靖匠此因以歸之弇
尊大文尤生朝日文邀倖束郎龅䚻堂
仲岑鞠日文邀倖束郎龅䚻堂
　張爰和

47. 江国纶垂图

清康熙四十八年（公元1709年）
王原祁
纸本设色
手卷
纵26、横146.1厘米
大都会艺术博物馆

Fishing in River Country at Blossom Time

Qing dynasty (1644–1911), dated 1709
Wang Yuanqi
Ink and color on paper
Handscroll
H×W : 26×146.1 cm
The Metropolitan Museum of Art
Bequest of John M. Crawford Jr., 1988

48. 山水图

清康熙四十九年（公元1710年）
王原祁
纸本设色
立轴
纵95.3、横47厘米
大都会艺术博物馆

Landscape

Qing dynasty (1644–1911), dated 1710
Wang Yuanqi
Ink and color on paper
Hanging scroll
H×W : 95.3×47 cm
The Metropolitan Museum of Art
Gift of Marie-Hélène Weill and Guy A. Weill, 2011

49. 辋川图

清康熙五十年（公元1711年）
王原祁
纸本设色
手卷
纵35.6、横545.5厘米
大都会艺术博物馆

Wangchuan Villa

Qing dynasty (1644–1911), dated 1711
Wang Yuanqi
Ink and color on paper
Handscroll
H×W : 35.6×545.5 cm
The Metropolitan Museum of Art
Ex coll.: C. C. Wang Family, Purchase,
Douglas Dillon Gift, 1977

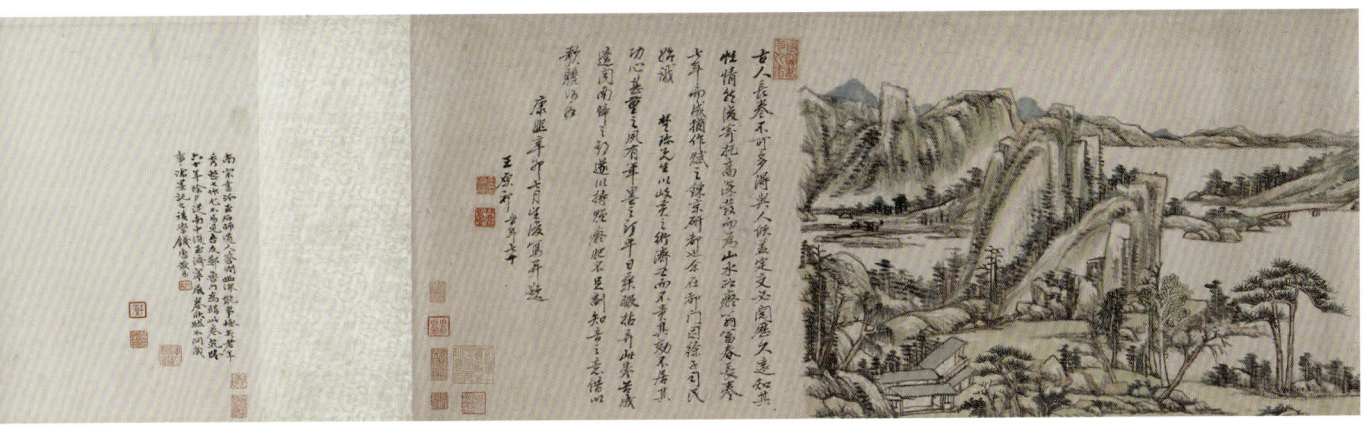

50. 严滩春晓图

清康熙五十年（公元1711年）
王原祁
纸本设色
手卷
纵39.3、横341.5厘米
波士顿美术博物馆

Spring Morning at Yanling Shoals

Qing dynasty (1644–1911), dated 1711
Wang Yuanqi
Ink and color on paper
Handscroll
H×W : 39.3×341.5 cm
The Museum of Fine Arts, Boston
Keith McLeod Fund
© 2024 Museum of Fine Arts, Boston

51. 仿黄公望山水图

清康熙五十一年（公元1712年）
王原祁
纸本设色
扇面
纵16.5、横49厘米
耶鲁大学艺术博物馆

Landscape After Huang Gongwang

Qing dynasty (1644–1911), dated 1712
Wang Yuanqi
Ink and color on paper
Fan
H×W : 16.5×49 cm
The Yale University Art Gallery
Archer M. Huntington, M.A. (Hon.) 1897, Fund

52. 仿倪瓒山水图

清
王原祁
纸本设色
立轴
纵80.4、横43.5厘米
克利夫兰美术馆

Landscape After Ni Zan

Qing dynasty (1644–1911)
Wang Yuanqi
Ink and color on paper
Hanging scroll
H×W : 80.4×43.5 cm
The Cleveland Museum of Art
John L. Severance Fund

53. 仿王蒙溪山行旅图

清
吴历
纸本水墨
立轴
纵59.1、横27厘米
大都会艺术博物馆

Travelers Among Streams and Mountains After Wang Meng

Qing dynasty (1644–1911)
Wu Li
Ink on paper
Hanging scroll
H×W : 59.1×27 cm
The Metropolitan Museum of Art
Ex coll.: C. C. Wang Family, Edward Elliott Family Collection, Purchase, The Dillon Fund Gift, 1981

54. 秋水图

清
吴历
纸本水墨
扇面
纵18、横53.9厘米
波士顿美术博物馆

River in Autumn

Qing dynasty (1644–1911)
Wu Li
Ink on paper
Fan
H×W : 18×53.9 cm
The Museum of Fine Arts, Boston
Chinese and Japanese Special Fund
© 2024 Museum of Fine Arts, Boston

55. 万壑松风图

清
（传）吴历
纸本设色
立轴
纵109.5、横25.9厘米
克利夫兰美术馆

Pine Wind from Myriad Villages

Qing dynasty (1644–1911)
Attributed to Wu Li
Ink and color on paper
Hanging scroll
H×W : 109.5×25.9 cm
The Cleveland Museum of Art
John L. Severance Fund 1954.584

56. 没骨牡丹图

清康熙二十四年（公元1685年）
恽寿平
绢本设色
立轴
纵18.4、横71.8厘米
克利夫兰美术馆

Peonies

Qing dynasty (1644–1911), dated 1685
Yun Shouping
Ink and color on silk
Hanging scroll
H×W : 18.4×71.8 cm
The Cleveland Museum of Art
Gift of the American Foundation for the Maud E. and Warren H. Corning Botanical Collection

57. 花卉图册

清
恽寿平
纸本设色
册页
每开：纵27.5、横43厘米
大阪市立美术馆

Flower Paintings

Qing dynasty (1644–1911)
Yun Shouping
Ink and color on paper
Album leaf
H×W(each leaf) : 27.5×43 cm
The Osaka City Museum of Fine Arts

116

58. 花卉图

清
恽寿平
纸本设色
扇面
纵17、横50.8厘米
大都会艺术博物馆

Carnations and Amaranthus

Qing dynasty (1644–1911)
Yun Shouping
Ink and color on paper
Fan
H×W : 17×50.8 cm
The Metropolitan Museum of Art
Bequest of John M. Crawford Jr., 1988

59. 冷艳含香图

清康熙二十七年（公元1688年）
（传）恽寿平
纸本设色
扇面
纵22.86、横50.8厘米
印第安纳波利斯艺术博物馆

Camellia and Wax Plum

Qing dynasty (1644–1911), dated 1688
Attributed to Yun Shouping
Ink and color on paper
Fan
H×W : 22.86×50.8 cm
The Indianapolis Museum of Art
Gift of the Alliance of the Indianapolis
Museum of Art, Miscellaneous Asian Art Fund

60. 仿钱选溪山早春图

清康熙三十五年（公元1696年）
杨晋
纸本设色
册页
纵31.4、横33.2厘米
耶鲁大学艺术博物馆

Stream and Mountain in Early Spring After Qian Xuan

Qing dynasty (1644–1911), dated 1696
Yang Jin
Ink and color on paper
Album leaf
H×W : 31.4×33.2 cm
The Yale University Art Gallery
Leonard C. Hanna, Jr., Class of 1913, Fund

61. 柳岸牧牛图

清康熙五十六年（公元1717年）
杨晋
纸本设色
立轴
纵99、横46.3厘米
耶鲁大学艺术博物馆

Buffalo on Willow Bank

Qing dynasty (1644–1911), dated 1717
Yang Jin
Ink and color on paper
Hanging scroll
H×W : 99×46.3 cm
The Yale University Art Gallery
Gift of Wango H. C. Weng

62. 仿李成古松图

清康熙五十五年（公元1716年）
黄鼎
绢本设色
立轴
纵199.2、横115.5厘米
耶鲁大学艺术博物馆

Old Pine After Li Cheng

Qing dynasty (1644–1911), dated 1716
Huang Ding
Ink and color on silk
Hanging scroll
H×W : 199.2×115.5 cm
The Yale University Art Gallery
Gift of Karen Wang

63. 山水图

清雍正六年（公元1728年）
（传）黄鼎
纸本水墨
手卷
纵48.8、横102厘米
科隆东亚艺术博物馆

Landscape

Qing dynasty (1644–1911), dated 1728
Attributed to Huang Ding
Ink on paper
Handscroll
H×W : 48.8×102 cm
The Museum of East Asian Art, Cologne
© Rheinisches Bildarchiv Köln

64. 松涛图

清康熙四十四年（公元1705年）
沈宗敬
绢本水墨
立轴
纵144.62、横49.69厘米
明尼阿波利斯美术馆

Soughing of Wind in Pines Echoes Melody of Spring

Qing dynasty (1644–1911), dated 1705
Shen Zongjing
Ink on silk
Hanging scroll
H×W : 144.62×49.69 cm
The Minneapolis Institute of Art
The Friends of Bruce Dayton Art Acquisition Fund

65. 春泉洗药图 | Cleansing Medicinal Herbs in Stream on Spring Day

清康熙四十二年（公元1703年）
禹之鼎
纸本设色
手卷
纵36.2、横132.5厘米
克利夫兰美术馆

Qing dynasty (1644–1911), dated 1703
Yu Zhiding
Ink and color on paper
Handscroll
H×W : 36.2×132.5 cm
The Cleveland Museum of Art
Severance and Greta Millikin Purchase Fund

66. 朱彝尊像

清	Portrait of Zhu Yizun
禹之鼎	Qing dynasty (1644–1911)
纸本设色	Yu Zhiding
立轴	Ink and color on paper
纵77.79、横41.75厘米	Hanging scroll
明尼阿波利斯美术馆	H×W : 77.79×41.75 cm
	The Minneapolis Institute of Art
	The Friends of Bruce Dayton Art Acquisition Fund

67. 寒林图

清康熙三十三年（公元1694年）
蔡远
纸本水墨
立轴
纵102.9、横49.8厘米
耶鲁大学艺术博物馆

Landscape with Wintry Trees

Qing dynasty (1644–1911), dated 1694
Cai Yuan
Ink on paper
Hanging scroll
H×W : 102.9×49.8 cm
The Yale University Art Gallery
Gift of Wango H. C. Weng

68. 仿李希古九如图

清康熙三十五年（公元1696年）
（传）蔡远
纸本设色
册页
纵32.9、横37.5厘米
耶鲁大学艺术博物馆

Landscape After Li Xigu

Qing dynasty (1644–1911), dated 1696
Attributed to Cai Yuan
Ink and color on paper
Album leaf
H×W : 32.9×37.5 cm
The Yale University Art Gallery
Gift of Wango H.C. Weng

69. 芍药图

清
上睿
绢本设色
立轴
纵70、横60.3厘米
波士顿美术博物馆

White Peonies

Qing dynasty (1644–1911)
Shang Rui
Ink and color on silk
Hanging scroll
H×W : 70×60.3 cm
The Museum of Fine Arts, Boston
Bequest of Charles Bain Hoyt—Charles Bain Hoyt Collection
© 2024 Museum of Fine Arts, Boston

70. 渡江图

清
上睿
纸本设色
立轴
纵96.2、横39.7厘米
克利夫兰美术馆

Crossing of Yangzi River

Qing dynasty (1644–1911)
Shang Rui
Ink and color on paper
Hanging scroll
H×W : 96.2×39.7 cm
The Cleveland Museum of Art
Gift of Wen Fong in honor of Philip Hoffer

71. 山水图

清
徐枋
纸本水墨
立轴
纵60.5、横33.5厘米
耶鲁大学艺术博物馆

Landscape

Qing dynasty (1644–1911)
Xu Fang
Ink on paper
Hanging scroll
H×W : 60.5×33.5 cm
The Yale University Art Gallery
Gift of Wango H. C. Weng

72. 山水图

明崇祯十六年（公元1643年）
祁豸佳
纸本水墨
册页
纵16.5、横49.5厘米
大都会艺术博物馆

Landscape

Late Ming to early Qing dynasty, dated 1643
Qi Zhijia
Ink on paper
Album leaf
H×W : 16.5×49.5 cm
The Metropolitan Museum of Art
John Stewart Kennedy Fund, 1913

73. 仿王蒙山水图

清康熙十九年（公元1680年）
祁豸佳
纸本设色
立轴
纵122、横54.7厘米
芝加哥艺术博物馆

Landscape After Wang Meng

Qing dynasty (1644–1911), dated 1680
Qi Zhijia
Ink and color on paper
Hanging scroll
H×W : 122×54.7 cm
The Art Institute of Chicago
Russell Tyson Fund
© 2024. The Art Institute of Chicago / Art Resource, NY/ Scala, Florence

74. 山水图

清
庄冏生
纸本水墨
扇面
纵16.2、横50.2厘米
大都会艺术博物馆

Landscape

Qing dynasty (1644–1911)
Zhuang Jiongsheng
Ink on paper
Fan
H×W : 16.2×50.2 cm
The Metropolitan Museum of Art
John Stewart Kennedy Fund, 1913

75. 黄檗宗僧侣群像

清
悦山道宗
纸本设色
立轴
纵171.5、横99.7厘米
克利夫兰美术馆

Portrait of Buddhist Monks of Obaku Sect

Qing dynasty (1644–1911)
Yueshan Daozong
Ink and color on paper
Hanging scroll
H×W : 171.5×99.7 cm
The Cleveland Museum of Art
Gift of Mr. and Mrs. Robert T. Gow

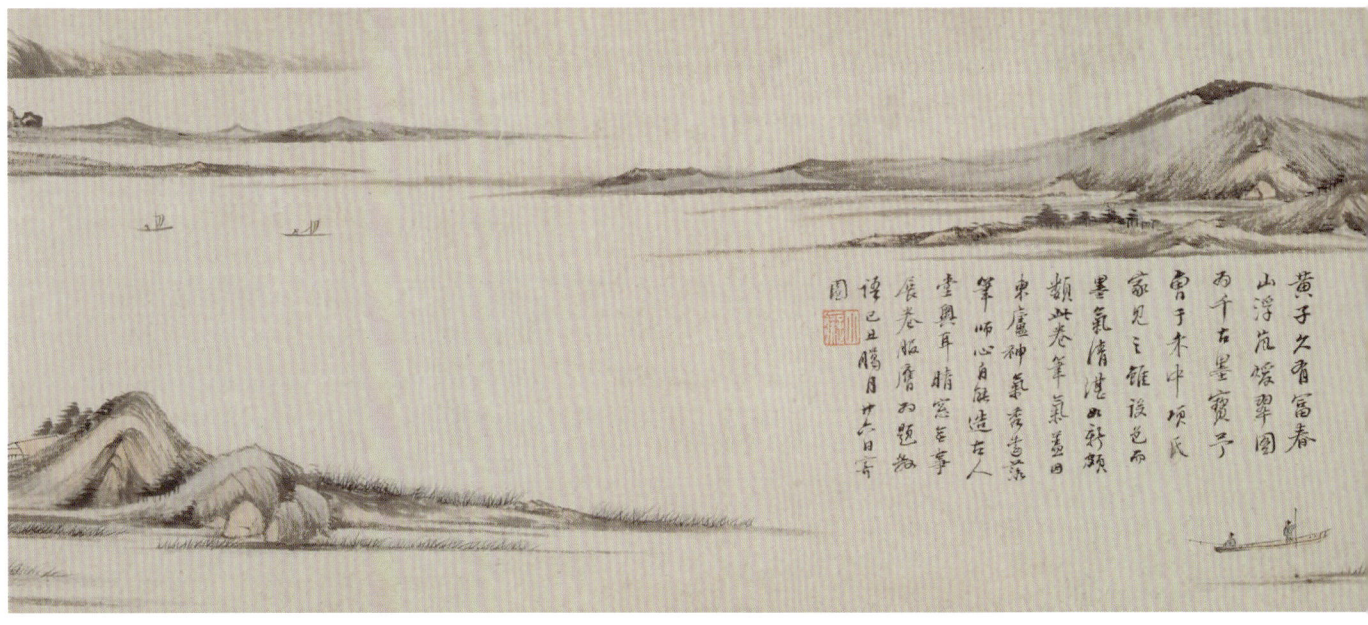

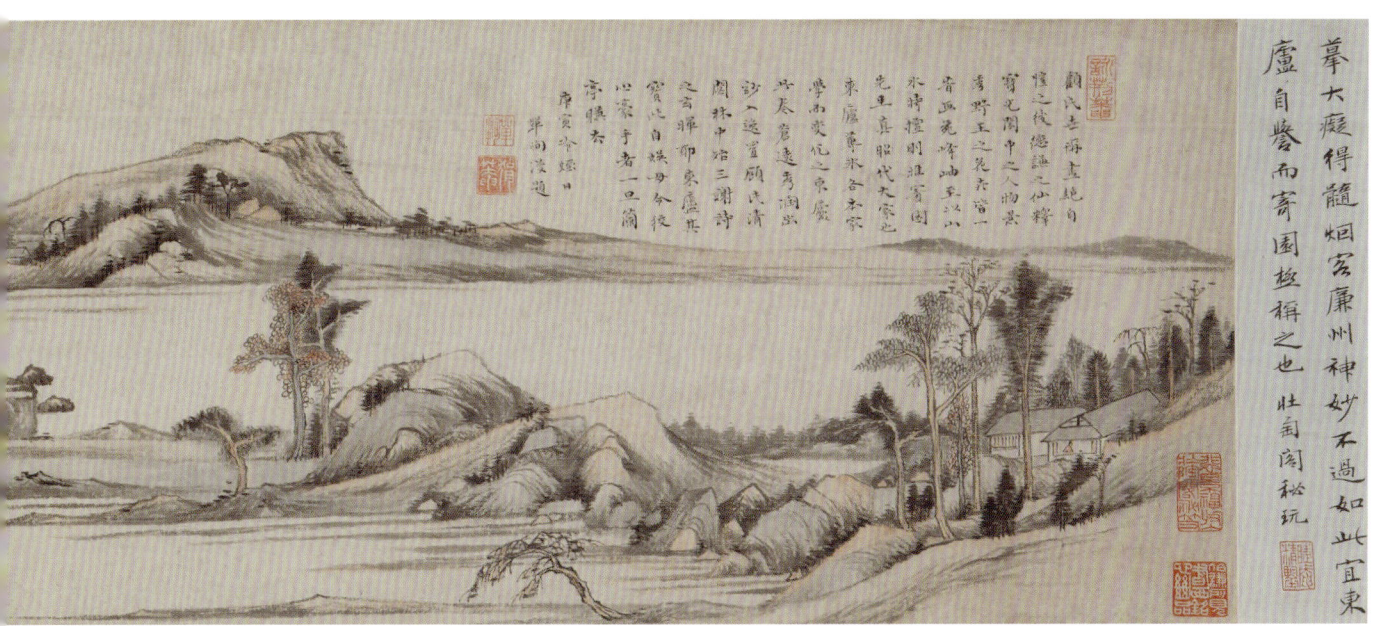

76. 仿黄公望浮岚暖翠图

清顺治六年（公元1649年）
顾天植
纸本设色
手卷
纵25.5、横717.5厘米
克利夫兰美术馆

Landscape After Huang Gongwang

Qing dynasty (1644–1911), dated 1649
Gu Tianzhi
Ink and color on paper
Handscroll
H×W: 25.5×717.5 cm
The Cleveland Museum of Art
John L. Severance Fund

此卷着色用筆邱壑全仿大癡浮嵐暖翠神
骨均肖但彼立軸此衍為長卷爾乙未秋景福記

顧夫植字東廬其下諸生鳳凰子山水專法元人
頃月光宇聞生就寄園松江入以李虎宧宜至郯其西法大癡
實探參以嘗邱屈然為藝林妙品
甲申初春伯韶浮此卷拈振鴻溪之奎畫軒因誌
此卷久藏近得大癡軸始知小癡跋不謬

慎伯論書謂二十年不能橫平豎直
蓋平直之難也如此魚之法通於書畫
竈用橫豎實無慶非用橫豎者東廬
此卷但能平直而能事老矣蓋能平
直則用筆細勁品有力車儆真
無乎不到未之宗賢昔合荷節讀此
卷深悟古人畫理 昔香光論寫樹以
為用筆宜曲至謂無有不曲者此所
謂曲自是寫樹法傾斜轉折靡其直角
在所謂平直者益非取界線之謂此理
尤易明也恐北香夫之說有觸豪用申
言之 庚申六月源暑汗下時
安吳胡韚城展讀竟日記

圖畫寶鑑續纂云顧天植字東廬松江華
生學乃卅寄園之山水蒼秀可嘉
庚申四月睫厂錄

77. 山水图

清
王无忝
纸本水墨
册页
纵20.3、横14.5厘米
集美博物馆

Landscape

Qing dynasty (1644–1911)
Wang Wutian
Ink on paper
Album leaf
H×W : 20.3×14.5 cm
The Guimet Museum
© RMN-Grand Palais (MNAAG, Paris) /
Thierry Ollivier

78. 山水图

清康熙九年（公元1670年）
章声
绢本设色
立轴
纵175.58、横95.89厘米
明尼阿波利斯美术馆

Landscape

Qing dynasty (1644–1911), dated 1670
Zhang Sheng
Ink and color on silk
Hanging scroll
H×W : 175.58×95.89 cm
The Minneapolis Institute of Art
Gift of funds from Joan Wurtele

79. 观瀑图

清康熙十八年（公元1679年）
章声
绢本设色
立轴
纵139.8、横37.4厘米
耶鲁大学艺术博物馆

Landscape with Waterfall

Qing dynasty (1644–1911), dated 1679
Zhang Sheng
Ink and color on silk
Hanging scroll
H×W : 139.8×37.4 cm
The Yale University Art Gallery
Bankers Trust Company Foundation, Karen Y. Wang Fund, and Asian Discretionary Fund

80. 仿高克恭山水图

清康熙十八年（公元1679年）
吕焕成
纸本设色
立轴
纵121.29、横61.44厘米
明尼阿波利斯美术馆

Landscape After Gao Kegong

Qing dynasty (1644–1911), dated 1679
Lv Huancheng
Ink and color on paper
Hanging scroll
H×W : 121.29×61.44 cm
The Minneapolis Institute of Art
The Shared Fund

81. 梅花书屋图

清康熙二十七年（公元1688年）
吕焕成
绢本设色
立轴
纵168.6、横91.5厘米
波士顿美术博物馆

Plum Blossom Studio

Qing dynasty (1644–1911), dated 1688
Lv Huancheng
Ink and color on silk
Hanging scroll
H×W : 168.6×91.5 cm
The Museum of Fine Arts, Boston
Gift of Edward Warren Bernat
© 2024 Museum of Fine Arts, Boston

82. 梅花图

清康熙九年（公元1670年）
文止
纸本设色
扇面
纵16.5、横50.2厘米
大都会艺术博物馆

Plum Blossoms

Qing dynasty (1644–1911), dated 1670
Wen Zhi
Ink and color on paper
Fan
H×W : 16.5×50.2 cm
The Metropolitan Museum of Art
John Stewart Kennedy Fund, 1913

83. 仿梅花道人山水图   **Landscape After Wu Zhen**

清康熙五年（公元1666年）
金俊明
纸本设色
扇面
纵17.8、横52.7厘米
哈佛艺术博物馆

Qing dynasty (1644–1911), dated 1666
Jin Junming
Ink and color on paper
Fan
H×W : 17.8×52.7 cm
The Harvard Art Museums
Harvard Art Museums/Arthur M. Sackler Museum, Asian Art Objects Fund
© President and Fel lows of Harvard College

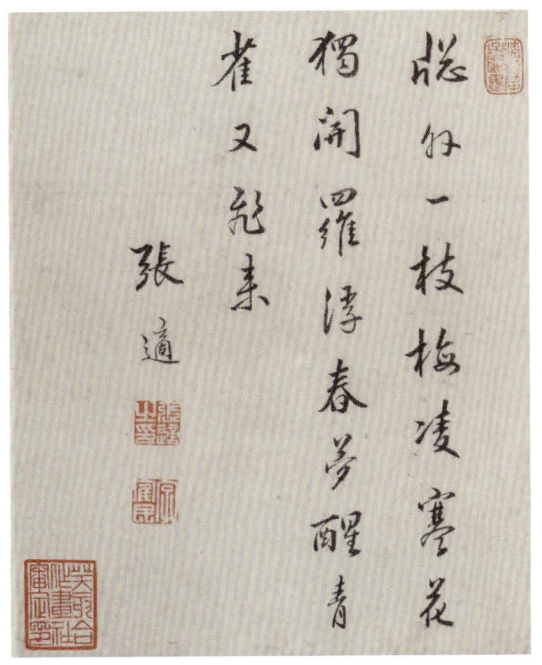

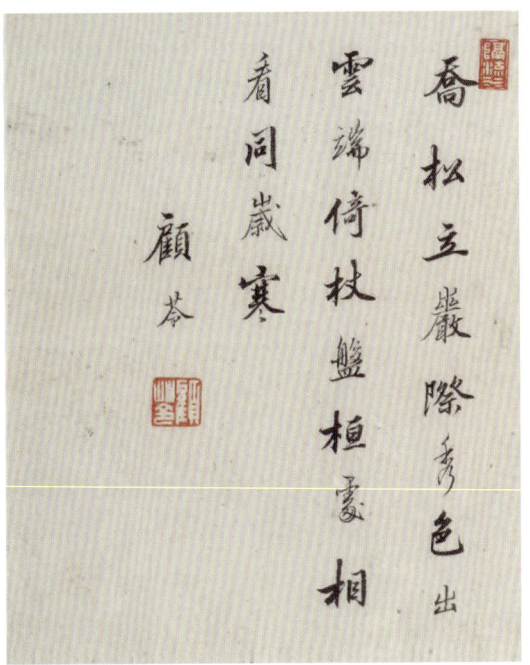
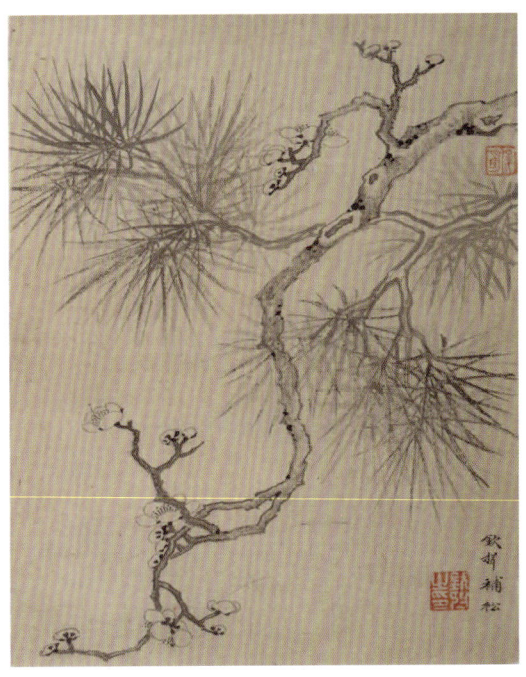

84. 梅花图册

清
金俊明
绢本设色
册页
每开：纵21.3、横16.5厘米
耶鲁大学艺术博物馆

Plum Blossoms

Qing dynasty (1644–1911)
Jin Junming
Ink and color on silk
Album leaf
H×W(each leaf) : 21.3×16.5 cm
The Yale University Art Gallery
Director's Discretionary Fund, Laura Seymour Doolittle Fund in memory of her sister Helen Wells Seymour, and Mr. and Mrs. Chauncey McCormick, B.A. 1907, Fund

窮冬多雪霰柔脆已
先摧不是丹砂質寧
能最後開

徐樹丕

花間春雪中態較
山茶小老圃為茶棋
命名端亦好

董俟

玉蝶舞衣紅相偎
白雲叢艷未留不佳
句引為春風

金俊明

萬卉迎春簇春殘花
點殘何當柔嫩且有
蒼看

朱陵

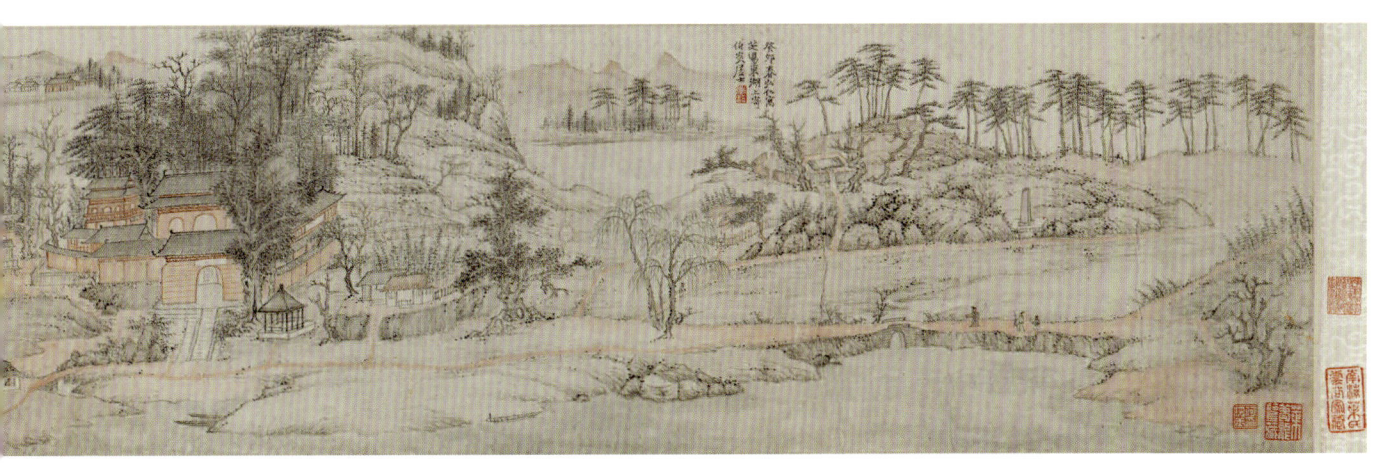

85. 芝易东湖图卷

清康熙二年（公元1663年）
弘仁
纸本设色
手卷
纵21.5、横101.7厘米
波士顿美术博物馆

Lake Zhiyang and Eastern Lake

Qing dynasty (1644–1911), dated 1663
Hong Ren
Ink and color on paper
Handscroll
H×W : 21.5×101.7 cm
The Museum of Fine Arts, Boston
Marshall H. Gould Fund
© 2024 Museum of Fine Arts, Boston

86. 断岗留别图

清
（传）弘仁
纸本水墨
立轴
纵69.5、横29.5厘米
科隆东亚艺术博物馆

Farewell

Qing dynasty (1644–1911)
Attributed to Hong Ren
Ink on paper
Hanging scroll
H×W : 69.5×29.5 cm
The Museum of East Asian Art, Cologne
© Rheinisches Bildarchiv Köln

拿天一徑許人通走壁泒根怪揩躬古柏瓊祠當與配

怪他容易出隆中卧龍松

奇光具大文海氣發天芬往昔應生悔于時若有聞

冠霞峯上日履濕磴中雲舉悟如歘牕孜孜競寸分

天門日上

天門者取道天都必躋此石門而上一徑南登則達峯頂先至天門後入
雲牖過一線天觀剔龍松作宜次於後予進時八月十九宿文殊院月色如晝
乘興半夜月下隨步幾天都峯囙有天門日上之作具全記中旼祥識

天門松
歷險到天門雙松
端以立今朝鬢皤
思植杖一顛撐
旼

87. 黄山八景图

清康熙二十年（公元1681年）
郑旼
纸本水墨
册页
每开：纵24.1、横14厘米
大都会艺术博物馆

Eight Views of Yellow Mountains

Qing dynasty (1616–1911), dated 1681
Zheng Min
Ink on paper
Album leaf
H×W(each leaf) : 24.1×14 cm
The Metropolitan Museum of Art
Purchase, The Vincent Astor Foundation Gift and Susan Dillon Gift, in honor of James C. Y. Watt, 2012

縣梯梁木接嶇嶔指定天南子午針巖洞中空沿出入風雷下界割晴陰縱觀六合思方廣誰鄭千秋不上尋此後躬行能造極無忘栗栗此時心登蓮峯絕頂作眩

仙橋我昔遠相望徑斷年深不可抗山中秘蹟應非少夢向天台渡石梁仙橋

不忿伶倫傳叔夜廣陵散絕到于今空山太古遺音在石上泉流響作琴鳴弦泉

仙橋拒鳴弦泉可十餘里可望而不可即導筆謂予自汪扶光先生到後徑斷多年矣因合圖之旺識

水土形墳任世傳雲程我自憶當年不迷襄野留岐閟未造倉書鳥篆先軒轅碑

潘生以素問刻入黄海誠非無見但墳索先乎五經秦火而後素問又豈能獨保乎然而其間若雜閏差月令諸篇市三典兩不及者不可不謂真古書斯儒者所當深究

旹紀事

倦遊於此憶廻腸津逮桃源若裸將九派清流泓可
掬郤如筵徹勸盈觴 九龍潭眎

何能跨鶴一躋攀自闢洪濛具古顏四面旋觀皆下拜分身千億散人間繞龍松旼

天都峯頌
將發陽川道中目有
里外遠觀尊巖巉
無復可登乃失焦三
百篇句頌之
倬彼靈溪岌極于天
維石嶷嶷巖乎萬斯
年攸莫不增方斷是
廣亦旣觀止隮則在
巘
辛酉秋七月畈畫并書

滄桑變盡人間世惟有天都尚古初絶壁固難攜蠟屐
烟蘿應得引霞裾閒情願早償塵俗極理終當賚玉
虛何日尋真能踐約石㕔丹鼎證倉書望天都峯
閱景升先生天都峯絶頂記非不能登登之惟艱耳予癸丑再入黄山
與汪子于晹實有皷勇之勝徐子孝則吳子顧卽坦阻之以畏險而且止不知
何年得償此夙願也畈并紀事

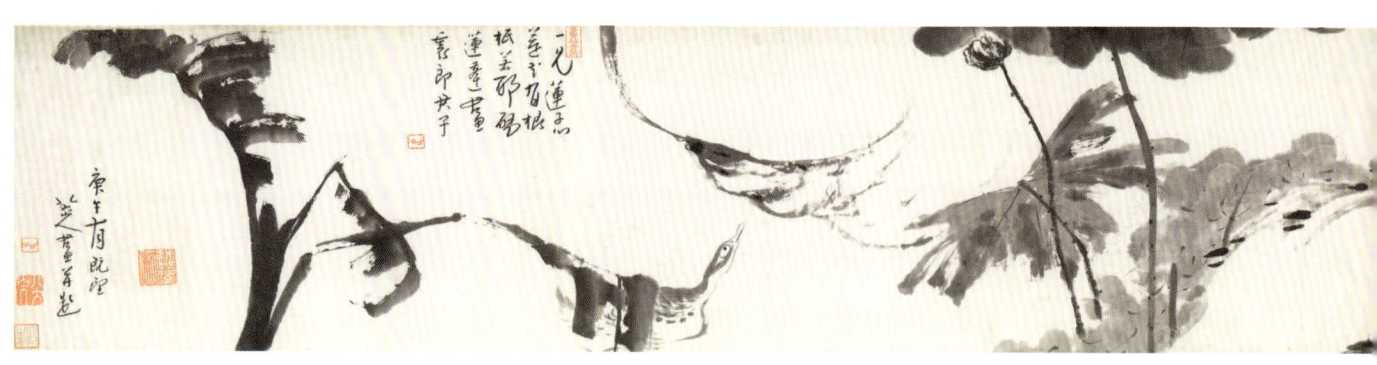

88. 荷塘花鸟图

清康熙二十九年（公元1690年）
朱耷
纸本水墨
手卷
纵39.1、横519.5厘米
辛辛那提艺术博物馆

Birds and Lotus Pond

Qing dynasty (1644–1911), dated 1690
Zhu Da
Ink on paper
Handscroll
H×W : 39.1×519.5 cm
The Cincinnati Art Museum
Museum Purchase 1950.79
© Bridgeman Images

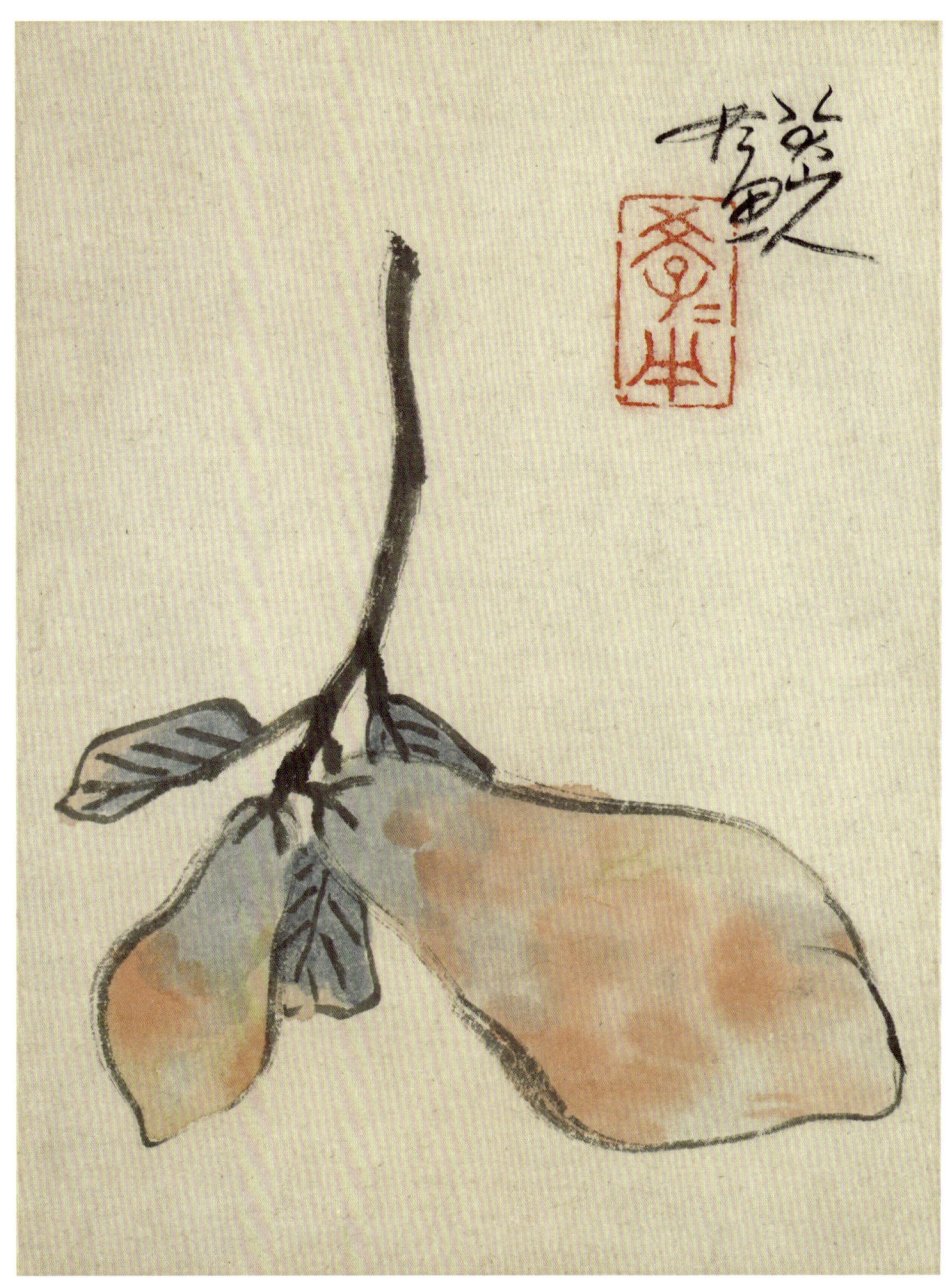

89. 木瓜图   **Quince**

清康熙二十九年（公元1690年）　Qing dynasty (1644–1911), dated 1690
朱耷　Zhu Da
纸本设色　Ink and color on paper
册页　Album leaf
纵20、横14.6厘米　H×W : 20×14.6 cm
普林斯顿大学美术馆　The Princeton University Art Museum
Museum purchase, Fowler McCormick, Class of 1921, Fund, in memory of Ellen B. Elliott
© 2024. Princeton University Art Museum/Art Resource NY/Scala, Florence

90. 菊花图

清康熙三十一年（公元1692年）
朱耷
纸本水墨
册页
纵22.5、横28.5厘米
科隆东亚艺术博物馆

Chrysanthemum

Qing dynasty (1644–1911), dated 1692
Zhu Da
Ink on paper
Album leaf
H×W : 22.5×28.5 cm
The Museum of East Asian Art, Cologne
© Rheinisches Bildarchiv Köln

91. 山水图册

清康熙三十八年（公元1699年）
朱耷
纸本设色
册页
每开：纵23.2、横18.7厘米
大都会艺术博物馆

Landscape Album

Qing dynasty (1644–1911), dated 1699
Zhu Da
Ink and color on paper
Album leaf
H×W(each leaf) : 23.2×18.7 cm
The Metropolitan Museum of Art
Bequest of John M. Crawford Jr., 1988

92. 鱼石图

清康熙三十八年（公元1699年）
朱耷
纸本水墨
立轴
纵135.3、横61厘米
大都会艺术博物馆

Fish and Rocks

Qing dynasty (1644–1911), dated 1699
Zhu Da
Ink on paper
Hanging scroll
H×W : 135.3×61 cm
The Metropolitan Museum of Art
Bequest of John M. Crawford Jr., 1988

93. 双鹰图

清康熙四十一年（公元1702年）
朱耷
纸本水墨
立轴
纵187.3、横90.2厘米
大都会艺术博物馆

Two Eagles

Qing dynasty (1644–1911), dated 1702
Zhu Da
Ink on paper
Hanging scroll
H×W : 187.3×90.2 cm
The Metropolitan Museum of Art
Ex coll.: C. C. Wang Family, Gift of Oscar L. Tang Family, 2014

94. 仿天池道人荷花图

清
朱耷
纸本水墨
立轴
纵186、横89.7厘米
波士顿美术博物馆

Lotus After Xu Wei

Qing dynasty (1644–1911)
Zhu Da
Ink on paper
Hanging scroll
H×W : 186×89.7 cm
The Museum of Fine Arts, Boston
Keith McLeod Fund
© 2024 Museum of Fine Arts, Boston

95. 仿郭恕先山水图

清
朱耷
纸本水墨
立轴
纵109.9、横56.4厘米
克利夫兰美术馆

Landscape After Guo Shuxian

Qing dynasty (1644–1911)
Zhu Da
Ink on paper
Hanging scroll
H×W : 109.9×56.4 cm
The Cleveland Museum of Art
John L. Severance Fund

96. 荷塘戏禽图

清
朱耷
绫本水墨
手卷
纵27.3、横205.1厘米
大都会艺术博物馆

Birds in Lotus Pond

Qing dynasty (1644–1911)
Zhu Da
Ink on satin
Handscroll
H×W : 27.3×205.1 cm
The Metropolitan Museum of Art
Bequest of John M. Crawford Jr., 1988

97. 渔石图

清
朱耷
纸本水墨
手卷
纵29.2、横157.4厘米
克利夫兰美术馆

Fish and Rocks

Qing dynasty (1644–1911)
Zhu Da
Ink on paper
Handscroll
H×W : 29.2×157.4 cm
The Cleveland Museum of Art
John L. Severance Fund 1953.247

98. 书画合册

清
朱耷
纸本水墨
册页
每开：纵25.4、横17.1厘米
弗利尔美术馆

Paintings and Calligraphies

Qing dynasty (1644–1911)
Zhu Da
Ink on paper
Album leaf
H×W(each leaf) : 25.4×17.1 cm
The Freer Gallery of Art
Bequest from the collection of Wang Fangyu and Sum Wai, donated in their memory by Mr. Shao F. Wang

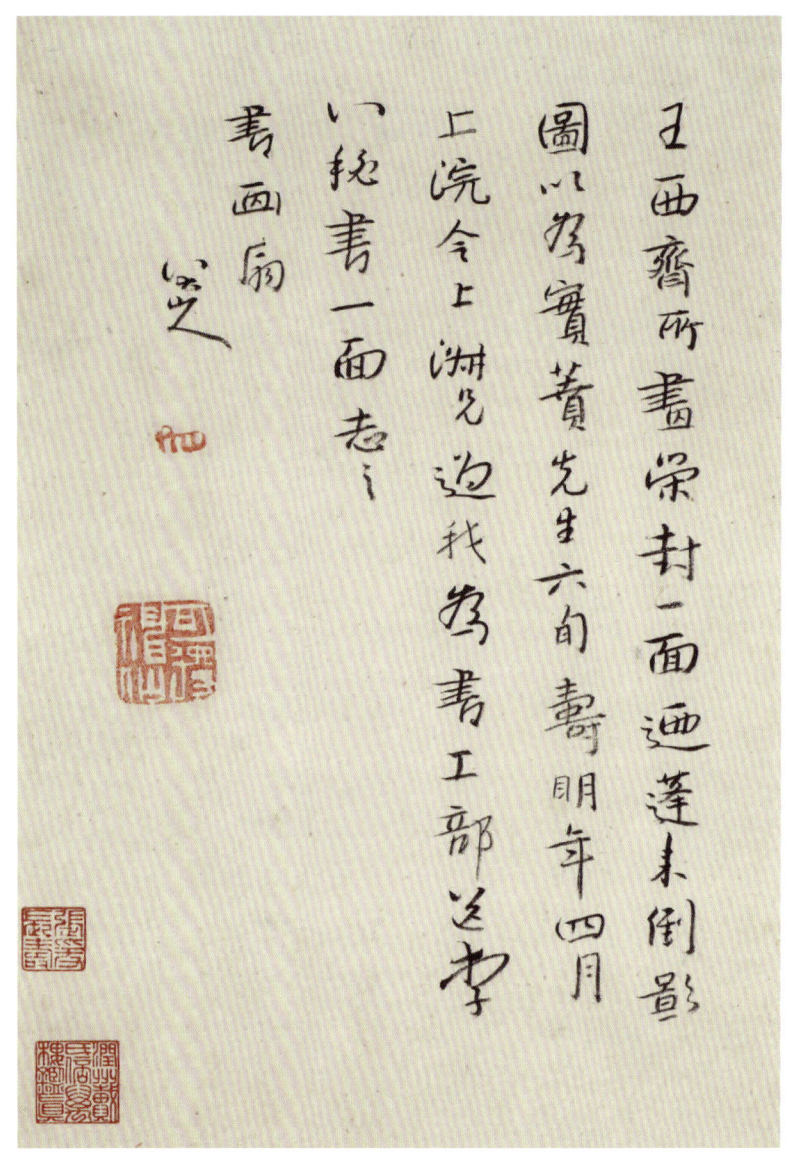

王西齋所畫榮封二面迺未倒影
圖以為寶養先生六旬壽期年四月
上浣令上淵兄迎我為書工部送李
八姪書一面志
書畫扇

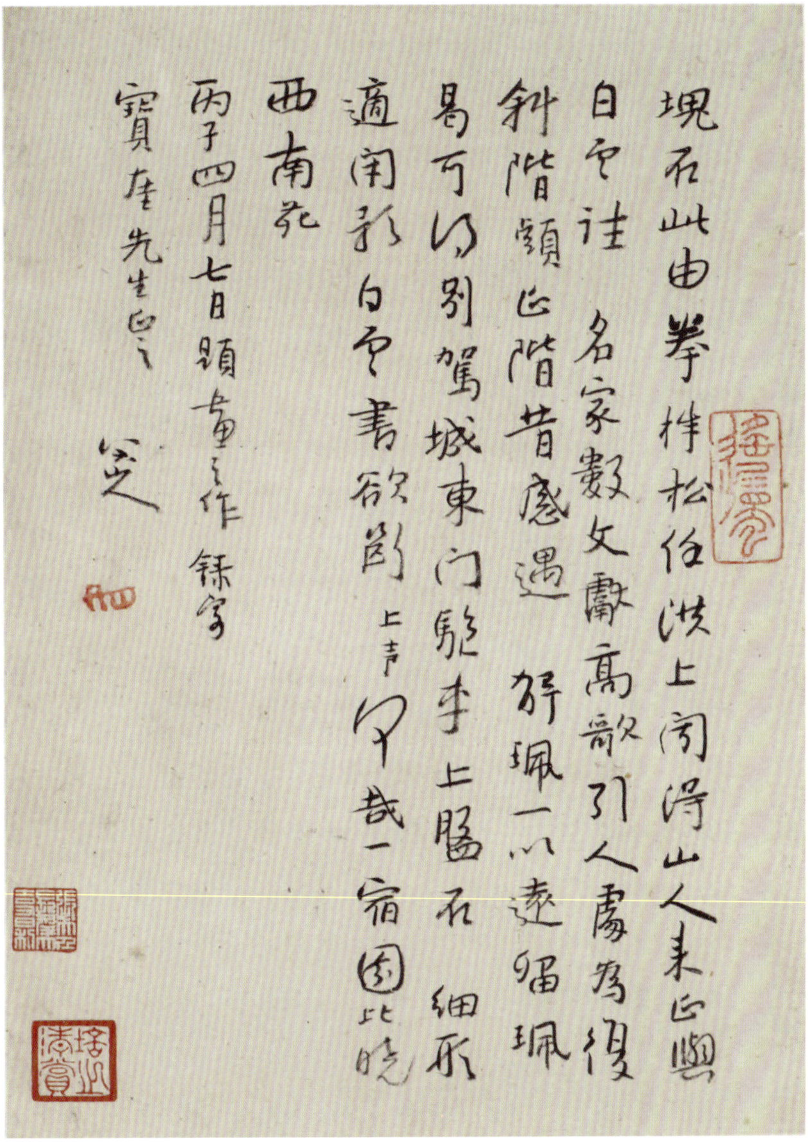
塊石此由拳拌松伯洪上閒得山人來正與
白雲往 名家數文獻高歌引人壽為復
斜階頭正階昔感遇 解珮一以遠猶珮
曷可以別駕城東門驍李上臨石 細聽
適聞彩白雲書欲斷（上声）卯哉一宿園此晚
西南花
丙子四月七日題董之作 錄寄
寶奎先生正之
適之

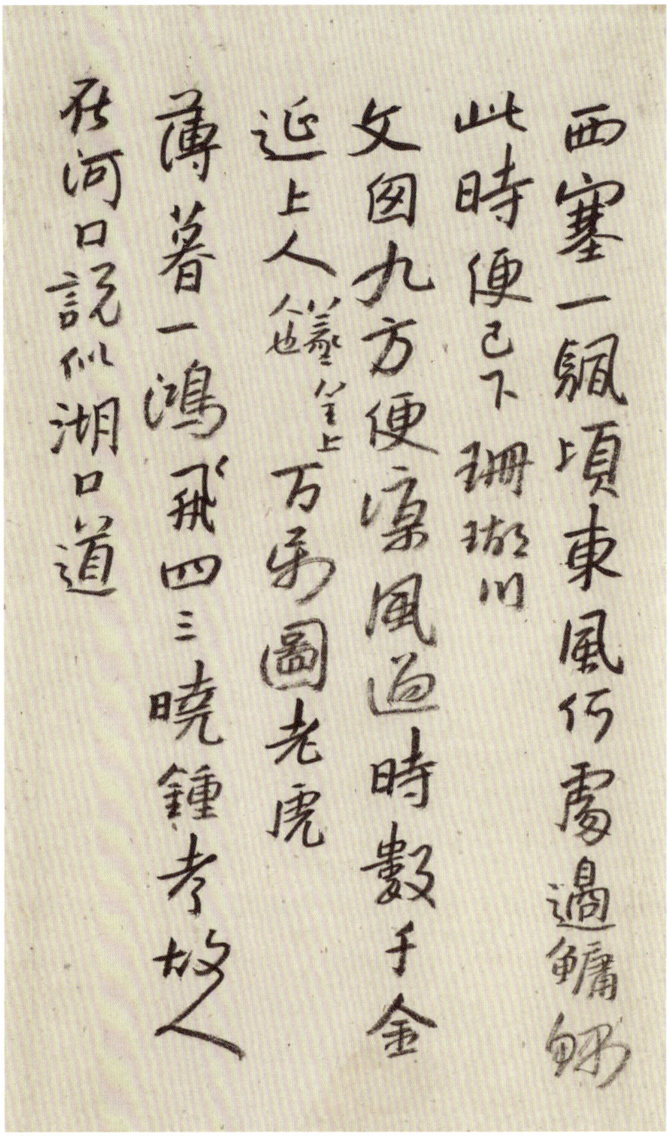

西塞一飆頂東風何處過鏞[illegible]

此時便己下珊瑚川

文圖九方便豪風過時數千金

近上人（鐩筌上人也）万象圖老虎

薄暮一鴻飛四三曉鐘考故人

於河口說似湖口道

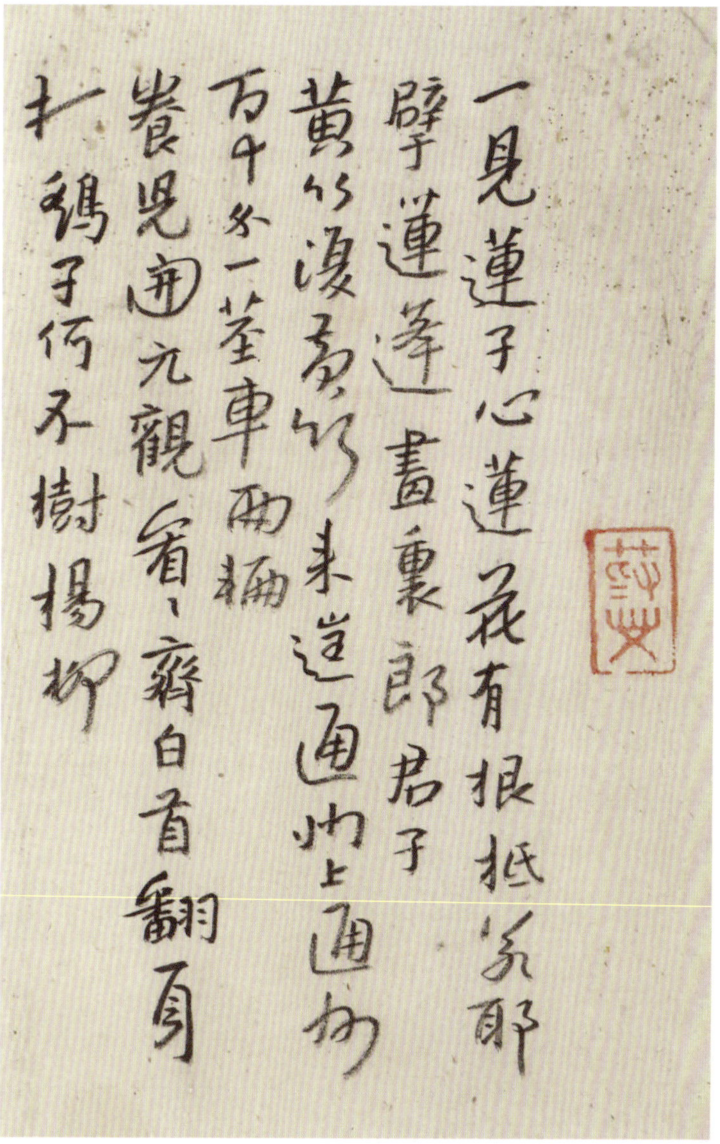

一見蓮子心蓮花有根抵禦郎
壁蓮逢畫裹郎君子
黃竹復黃竹未造通州上通州
万千外一莖車兩桶
養兒須九觀看、齊白首翻頁
扑鴉子何不樹揚柳

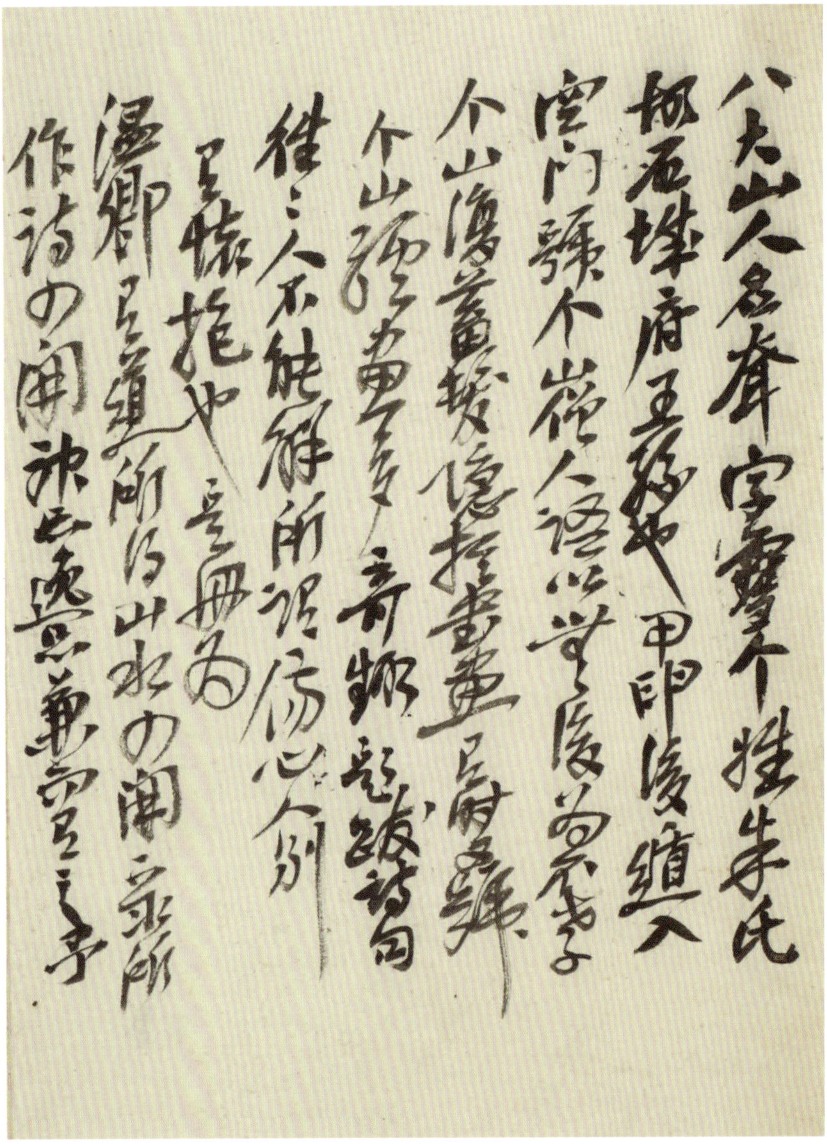

八大山人名奔字雪个姓朱氏
初居埧府王孫也甲申後遁入
空門頗不耐人語以筆代舌落筆
个山澹盪真饒隱括畫畫馬驢
个山證外書寫亦頗踈玩
住二不施衽所頊僞忽以別
号俸抱㝎㝎曲所
湯郷二直所乃山水の閗衆所
作詩の閗神出鬼没萬象呈于

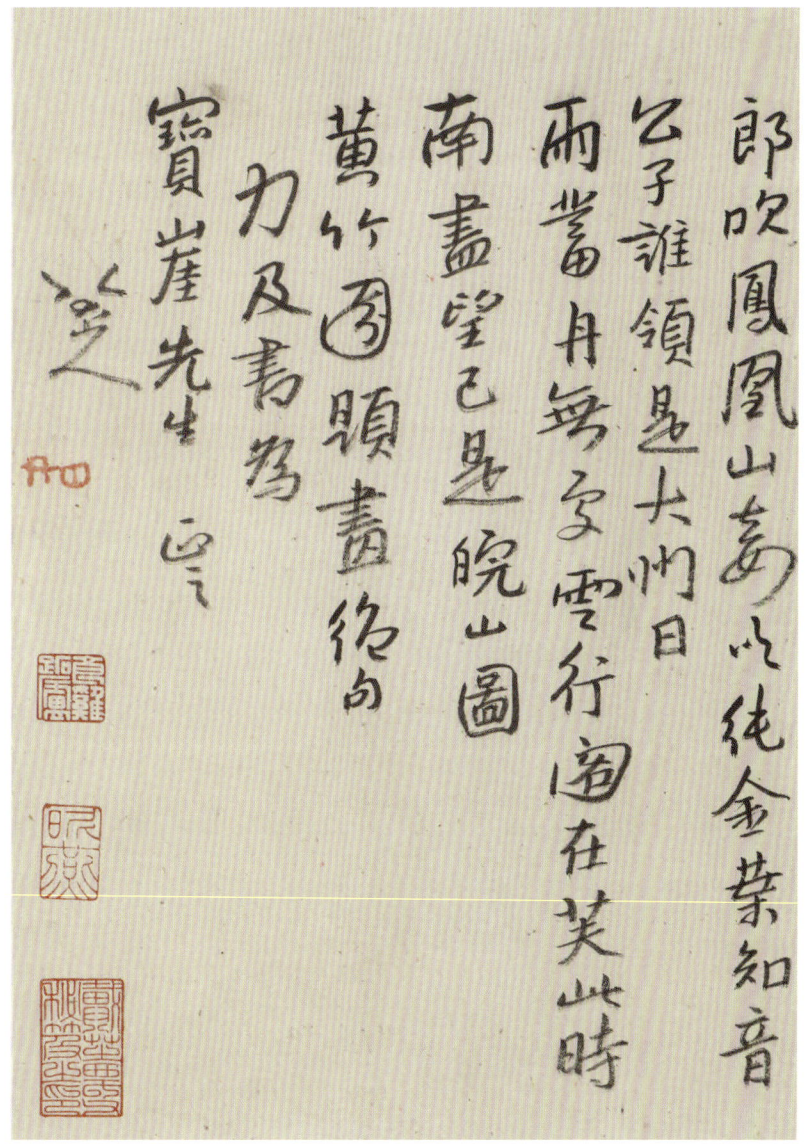

郎吹鳳凰山高以純金葉知音
公子誰領是大卅日
而當丹無字雲行囿在芙此時
南畫望已是皖山圖
黃竹圖題畫絕句
力及書為
寶崖先生正

芝

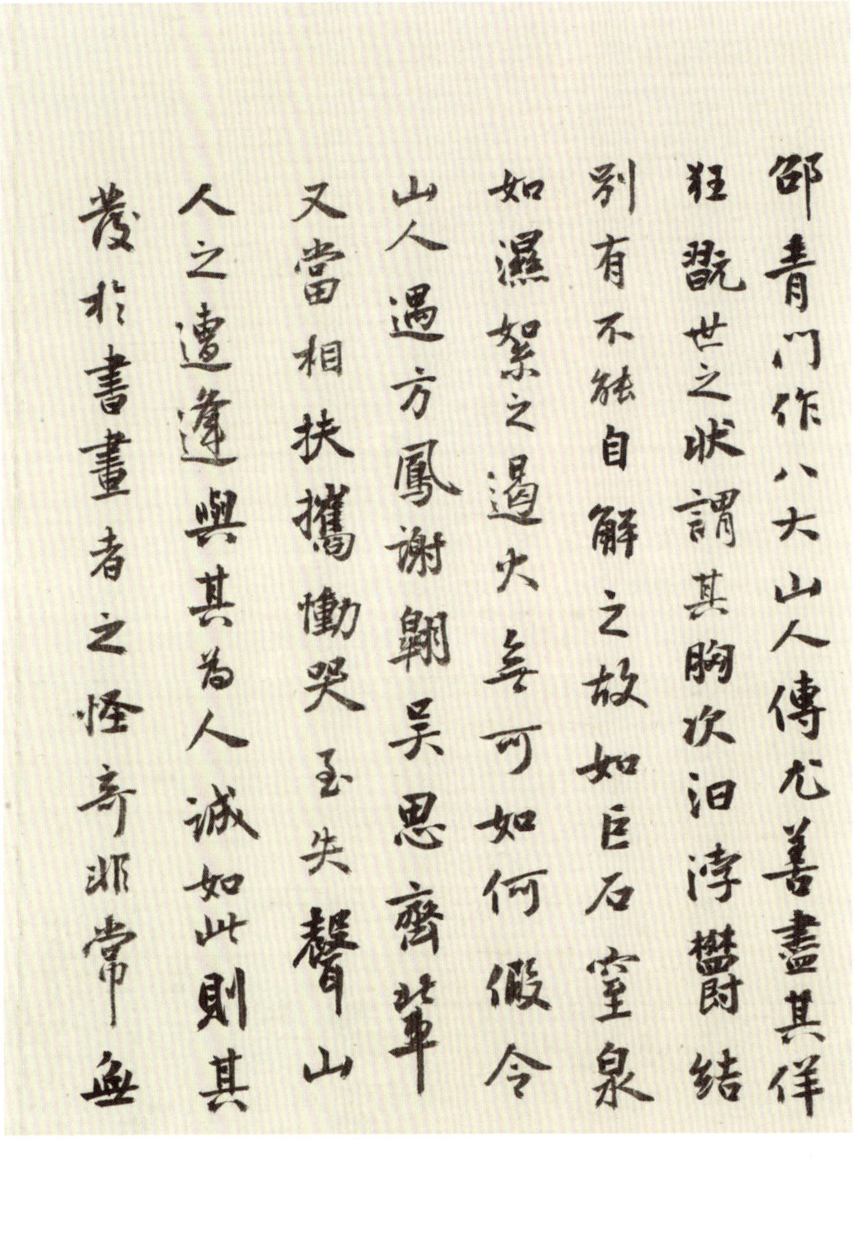

邵青門作八大山人傳尤善畫其佯
狂翫世之狀謂其胸次汩淳鬱結
別有不能自解之故如巨石窒泉
如濕絮之遏火無可如何假令
山人遇方鳳謝翺吳思齋輩
又當相扶攜慟哭玉失聲山
人之遭逢與其為人誠如此則其
發於書畫者之怪奇邪常無

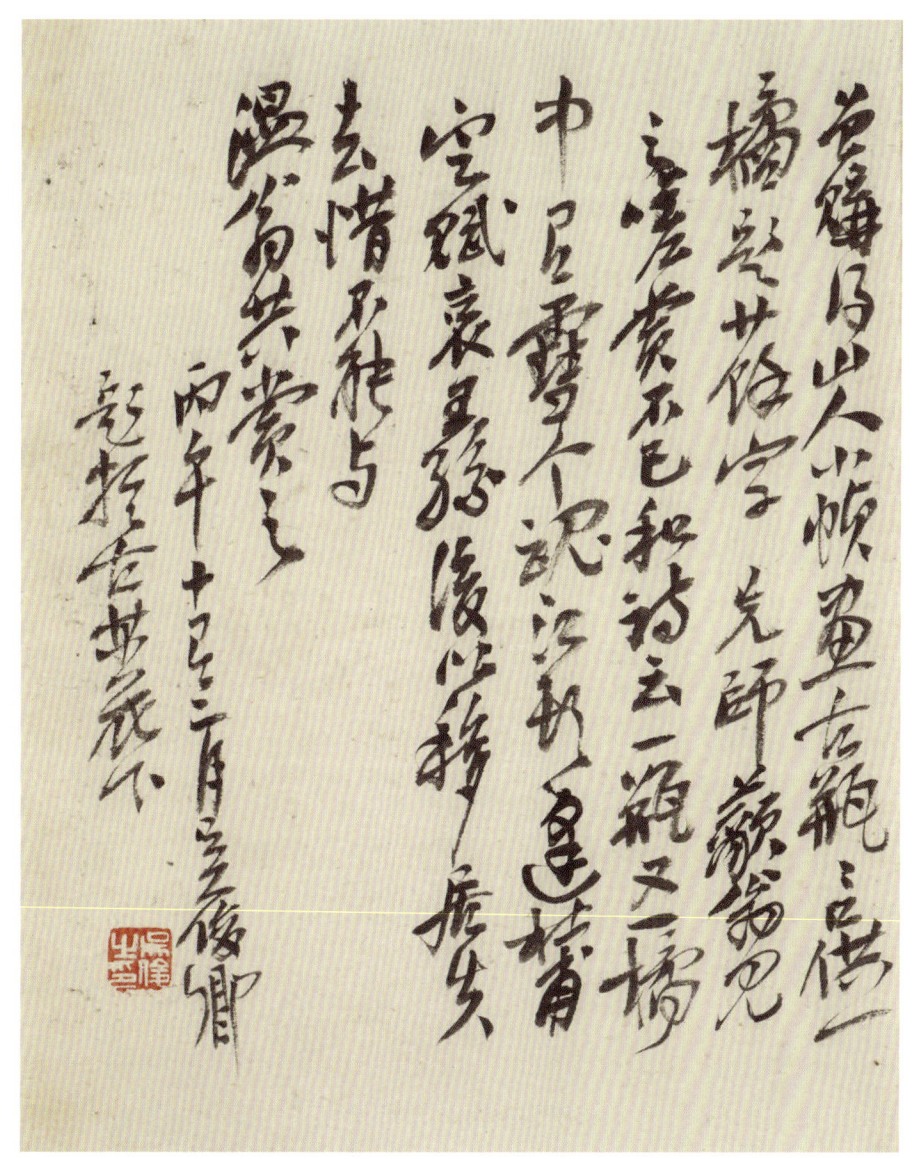

嘱使余題其後因書
昭和庚午八月 内藤虎

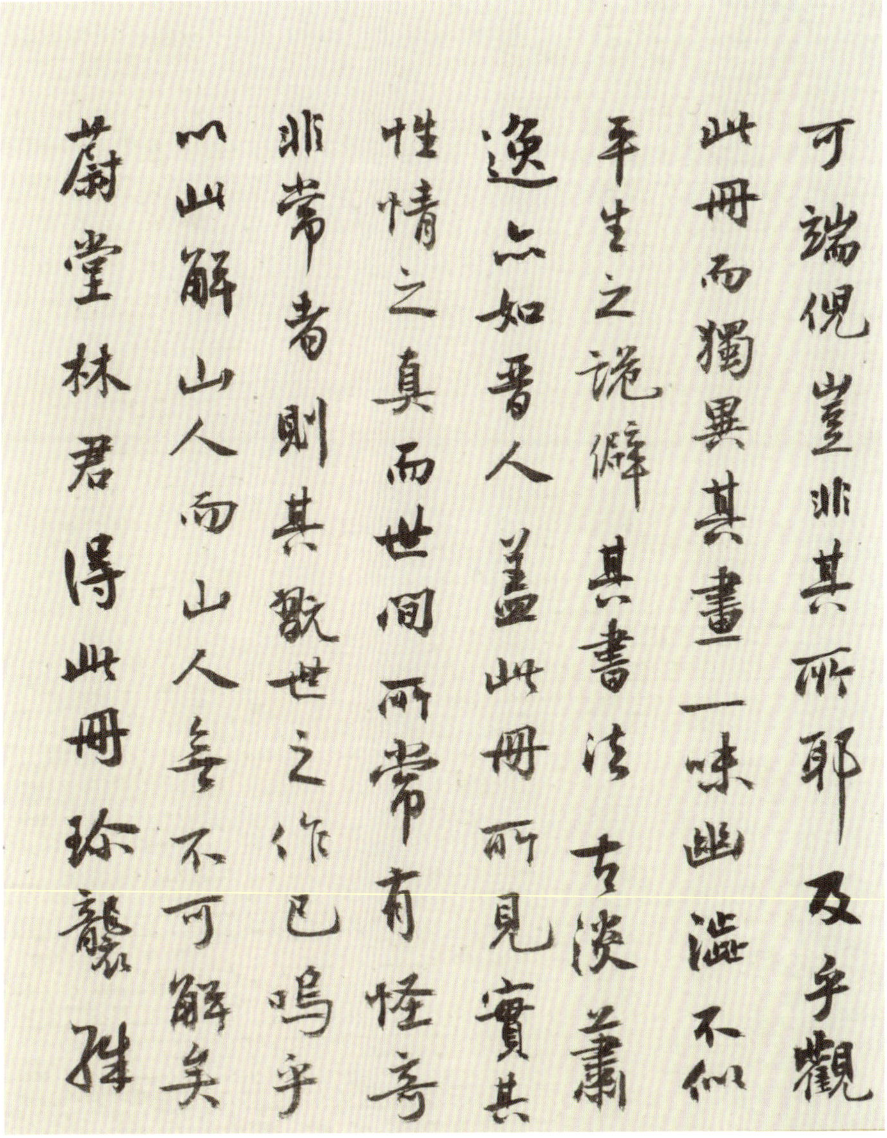

可端倪豈非其所耶及乎觀
此冊而獨異其畫一味幽澹不似
平生之詭僻其書法古澹蕭
逸亦如晉人蓋此冊所見實其
性情之真而世間所常有怪奇
非常者則其戲世之作已嗚乎
以此解山人而山人豈不可解矣
蔚堂林君得此冊珍襲拜

99. 草虫花卉图册

清
朱耷
纸本水墨
册页
尺寸不详
普林斯顿大学美术馆

Flowers and Insects

Qing dynasty (1644–1911)
Zhu Da
Ink on paper
Album leaf
Dimensions unknown
The Princeton University Art Museum
Gift of Mrs. George Rowley in memory of
Professor George Rowley
© 2024. Princeton University Art Museum/Art Resource NY/Scala, Florence

写竹写兰吴仲圭 何佩短竹蕙齐还家宗
远思壶子衔意狂张祗 马骅

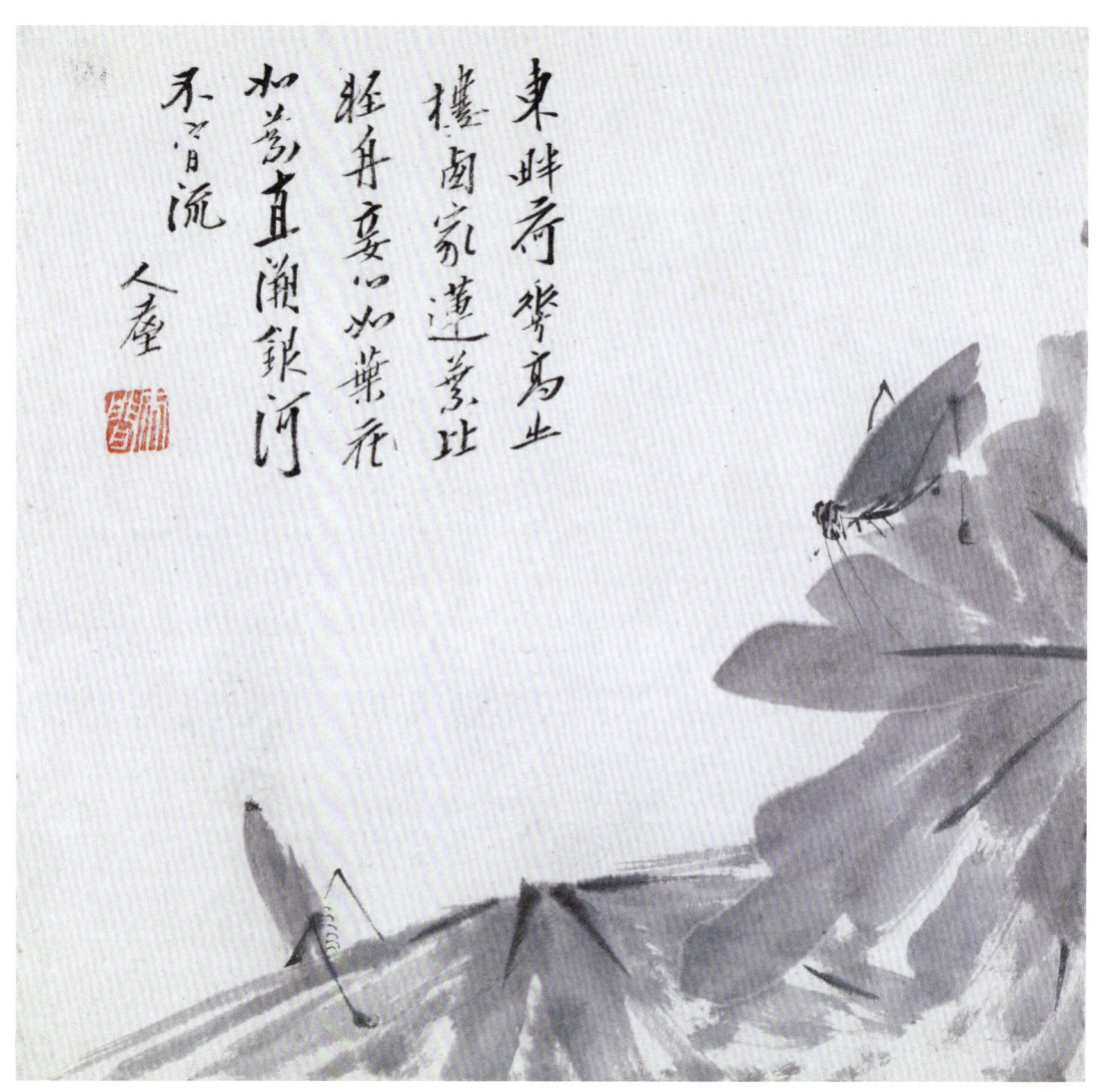

東畔荷蕖為業
檻南家蓮葉比
輕舟妾心如葉飛
如夢直瀕銀河
不日流
人窰

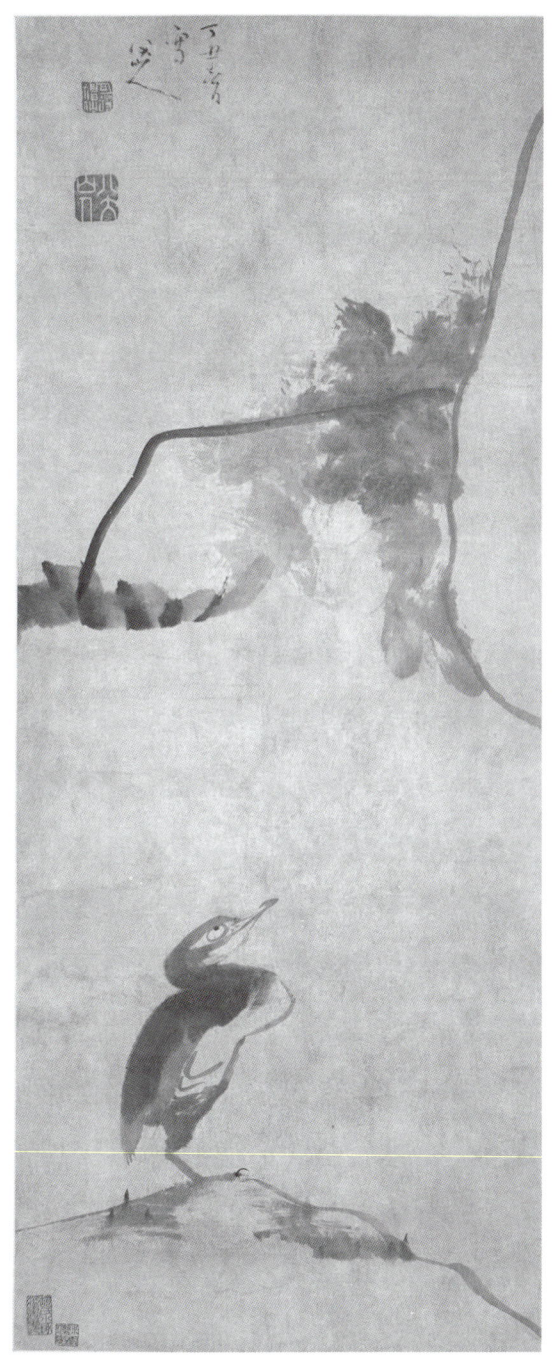

100. 荷花水禽图

清康熙三十六年（公元1697年）
（传）朱耷
纸本水墨
立轴
纵95.6、横37.5厘米
芝加哥艺术博物馆

Lotus and Waterfowl

Qing dynasty (1644–1911), dated 1697
Attributed to Zhu Da
Ink on paper
Hanging scroll
H×W : 95.6×37.5 cm
The Art Institute of Chicago
Buckingham Fund
© 2024. The Art Institute of Chicago / Art Resource, NY/ Scala, Florence

劉郎調側沅郎傅
富樾咸渡責挫姆
无更清平降皆玉
宋千十二有迴旋
芝菲昍

從未五色源頭水如此
天工水淡時畫与傾城
弄傾國莽間拜口天
兮箕
芝

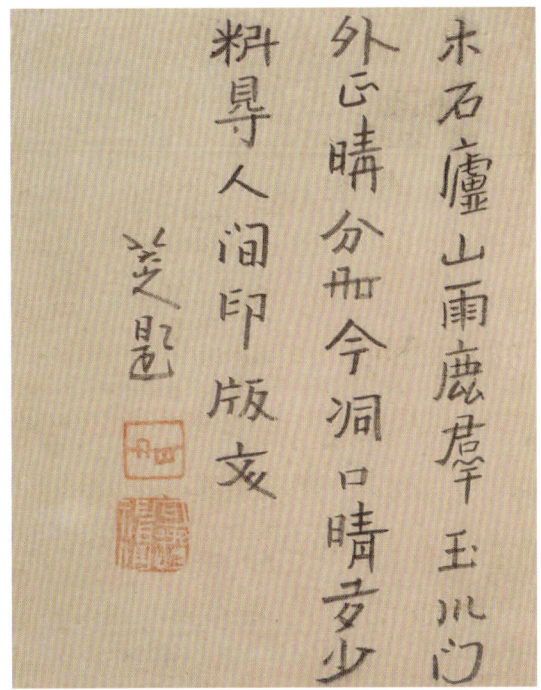

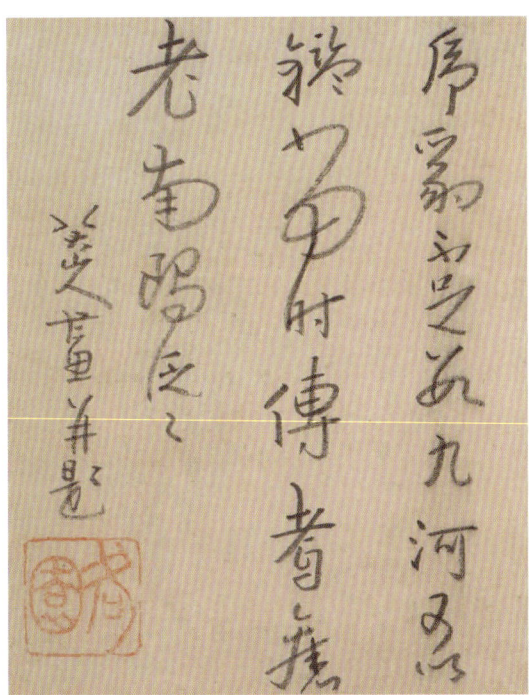

101. 诗画图册

清
（传）朱耷
纸本水墨
册页
每开：纵19.7、横15.2厘米
大都会艺术博物馆

Paintings and Poems

Qing dynasty (1644–1911)
Attributed to Zhu Da
Ink on paper
Album leaf
H×W(each leaf) : 19.7×15.2 cm
The Metropolitan Museum of Art
Seymour Fund, 1954

為爾千忠為爾一
人手無柯柯詞之
棄海盃粒浮

芝并題

朝上考慕青青
宫临泓下趁他井
出翻一外兩孫子

芝

薄暮雲山中 頗覺山家少 山家却近
遠樹 我不知老

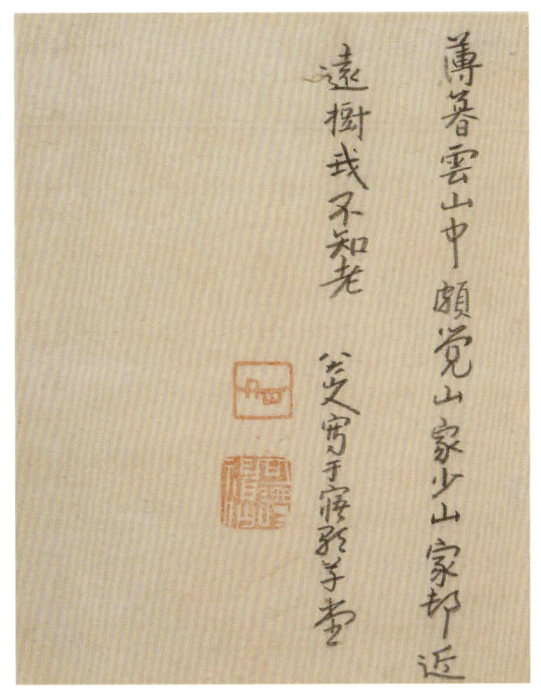

艸夾舠子方
彭搖雨、風
湖上橋 蓮
葉花房曾
塘去樂兒
鴰 芝

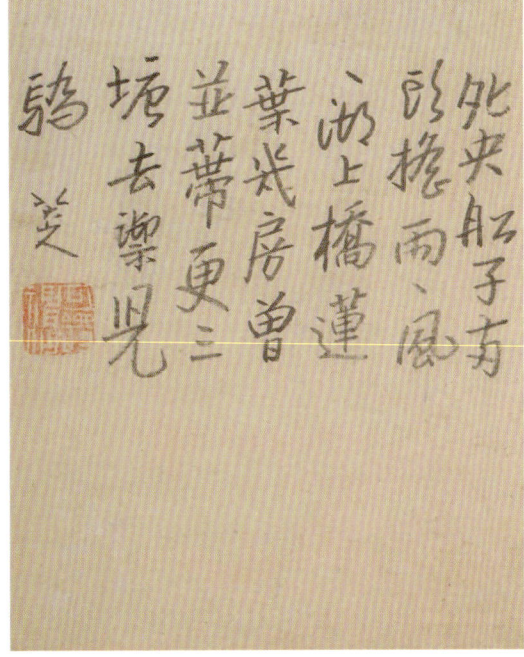

文宗之畫丹毛止上
河北董甘
玉局奉梨花吟
諸詩
芝

蒼崖飛瀑与高人高
與鶴寫鷄活句
如用蕉庐山亦
芝畫芳晶

玉匕葡萄酒一
尾屏開老李
復何為銅雀
當年使年少
韋公都長白元
雄
芝

西望一帆吃東風今
雪重鷹鷂此時便
已卜珊瑚
川
芝

承七月沙
子芝

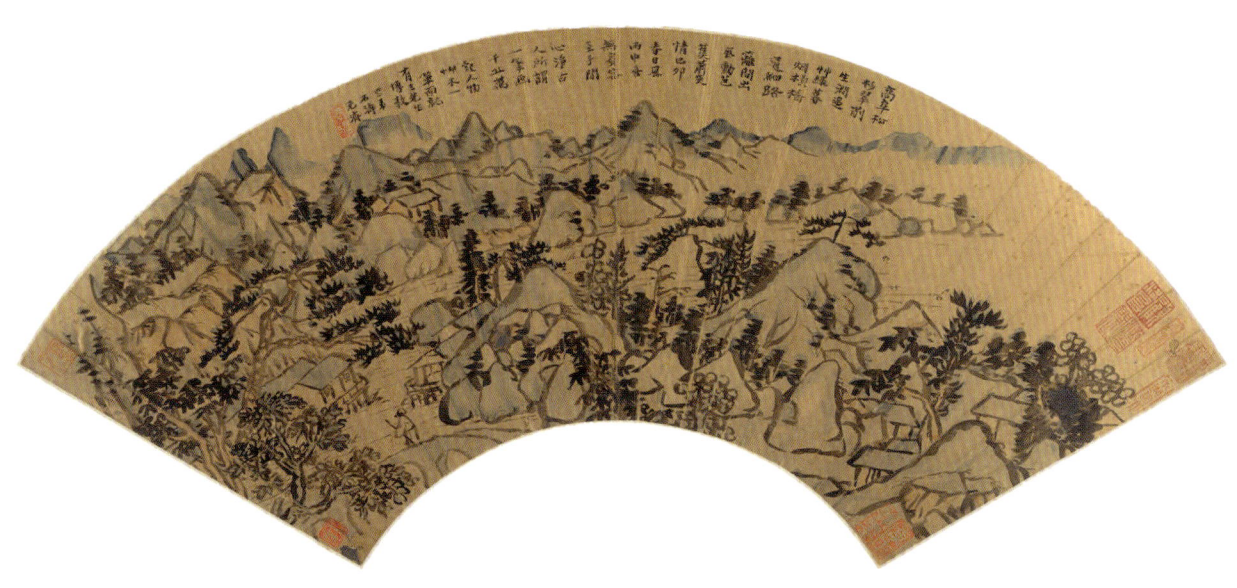

102. 山水图

清康熙三十八年（公元1699年）
（传）朱耷
纸本水墨
扇面
纵17.5、横44.5厘米
大都会艺术博物馆

Landscape

Qing dynasty (1644–1911), dated 1699
Attributed to Zhu Da
Ink on paper
Fan
H×W : 17.5×44.5 cm
The Metropolitan Museum of Art
Bequest of John M. Crawford Jr., 1988

103. 四鱼图

清
牛石慧
纸本水墨
扇面
纵38.1、横55.88厘米
印第安纳波利斯艺术博物馆

Four Fish

Qing dynasty (1644–1911)
Nlu Shihui
Ink on paper
Fan
H×W : 38.1×55.88 cm
The Indianapolis Museum of Art
Purchased to complement the Mr. and Mrs. Eli Lilly Collection of Chinese art through the bequest of Mrs. Enid Goodrich and the support of Lilly Endowment Inc.

版权支持

（按中文馆名音序排列）

鲍尔基金会鲍氏东方艺术馆
贝纳基博物馆
波士顿艺术博物馆
不列颠博物馆
大阪市立东洋陶瓷美术馆
大阪市立美术馆
大都会艺术博物馆
东京国立博物馆
费城艺术博物馆
菲尔德博物馆
弗利尔美术馆
弗利尔与赛克勒美术馆
哈佛艺术博物馆
荷兰国立博物馆
集美博物馆
金贝尔艺术博物馆
凯布朗利博物馆
克利夫兰艺术博物馆
科隆东亚艺术博物馆
洛杉矶郡艺术博物馆
明尼阿波利斯美术馆
奈良国立博物馆
普林斯顿大学美术馆
赛克勒博物馆
赛克勒美术馆
圣路易斯艺术博物馆
维多利亚和阿尔伯特博物馆
新南威尔士州美术馆
辛辛那提艺术博物馆
亚洲文明博物馆
耶鲁大学艺术博物馆
印第安纳波利斯艺术博物馆
芝加哥艺术博物馆

Image Contributors

(In Chinese Pinyin Order)

The Baur Foundation, Museum of Far Eastern Art

The Benaki Museum

The Museum of Fine Arts, Boston

The British Museum

The Museum of Oriental Ceramics, Osaka

The Osaka City Museum of Fine Arts

The Metropolitan Museum of Art

The Tokyo National Museum

The Philadelphia Museum of Art

The Field Museum

The Freer Gallery of Art

The Freer and the Arthur M. Sackler Gallery

The Harvard Art Museums

The Rijksmuseum

The Guimet Museum

The Kimbell Art Museum

The Quai Branly Museum

The Cleveland Museum of Art

The Museum of East Asian Art, Cologne

The Los Angeles County Museum of Art

The Minneapolis Institute of Art

The Nara National Museum

The Princeton University Art Museum

The Arthur M. Sackler Museum

The Arthur M. Sackler Gallery

The Saint Louis Art Museum

The Victoria and Albert Museum

The Art Gallery of New South Wales

The Cincinnati Art Museum

The Asian Civilisations Museum

The Yale University Art Gallery

The Indianapolis Museum of Art

The Art Institute of Chicago

编辑、出版人员

总 策 划　马汝军　谢　刚
选题策划　孙志鹏
主任编辑　邹懿男
出版统筹　丁　宁

责任编辑　李文彧　林　琳
特约编辑　丁文文
编　　辑　陈　雯　张小君　汪　欣　孙立英　白华召　施　然　马　源
　　　　　赵笑笑　刘　琦　黄　艳　王　萌　王颖洁　王宏亮　毕力格图
责任校对　刘　义
实习编辑　齐倩颖　潘泓瑾

英文翻译　丁文文　耿玮浩
英文审校　韩　华

装帧设计　冷暖儿
图文版式　魏　丹　杨　丹　阮鸽鸽
责任印制　韦　舰　李珊珊

Editorial Staff

Chief Publisher　Ma Rujun　Xie Gang

Publisher　Sun Zhipeng

Editorial Director　Zou Yinan

Publishing Coordinator　Ding Ning

Editors-in-Charge　Li Wenyu　Lin Lin

Contributing Editor　Ding Wenwen

Editors　Chen Wen　Zhang Xiaojun　Wang Xin　Sun Liying　Bai Huazhao　Shi Ran　Ma Yuan　Zhao Xiaoxiao　Liu Qi　Huang Yan　Wang Meng　Wang Yingjie　Wang Hongliang　Biligt

Responsible Proofreader　Liu Yi

Interns　Qi Qianying　Pan Hongjin

English Translators　Ding Wenwen　Geng Weihao

English Proofreader　Han Hua

Cover Designer　Leng Nuaner

Layout Designers　Wei Dan　Yang Dan　Ruan Gege

Responsible Printing Coordinators　Wei Jian　Li Shanshan